Couture Fabrics of the 50s

Joy Shih

4880 Lower Valley Road, Atglen, PA 19310

To Cindy Smith Shih
my sister - my friend
You wear your art so well

Published by Schiffer Publishing Ltd.
4880 Lower Valley Road
Atglen, PA 19310
Phone: (610) 593-1777
Fax: (610) 593-2002
E-mail: schifferbk @ aol.com

Please write for a free catalog.
This book may be purchased from the publisher.
Please include $2.95 for shipping.
Try your bookstore first.

We are interested in hearing from authors
with book ideas on related subjects.

Contents

Introduction

The beautiful French designer fabrics of the 1950s on these pages will leave you wanting for more. The floral, geometric, and novelty designs are printed and/or woven into the finest silks, rayon, linen and cottons. Unlike everyday wear, designer textiles of the era featured exquisite detailing using gold and irridescent accents, fabulous weaves, and innovative patterns. Artistic interpretations range from abstract design, a new wave in the 1950s, to special effects *trompe l'oeil* images, imitation weaves and textures. These textiles were used in tailored fashion wear for special or formal occasions, and were made available to couture houses on a seasonal basis. Some designs were also used for home decorating.

The fabric swatches are taken from actual pattern books from Parisian designer textile manufacturers. They are categorized by design in floral, geometric and novelty patterns. Though the fabric swatches are small and do not show repeats, information about overall design patterns are available in some cases through design sketches and are described if known. Each swatch is dated with reference to the design season and year from mid-decade to the late 1950s, and includes the general fiber such as silk, rayon, cotton, or linen. Additional information as to the type of silk, for example, are listed if known. Descriptions in quotation marks are translated from French. Actual French terms are indicated by italic text.

Floral designs in the book are arranged from abstract to realistic. Abstract art was all the rage in the 1950s and it is interesting to see the many interpretations of florals. With couture fabrics, there does not seem to be a standard for color schemes or design styles. Watercolor abstracts, for example, were available in muted grays, neutrals, and pastels as well as in intense royal blues, orange, red, and turquoise. Unlike everyday textiles, fashion fabrics usually are presented in one design, and not many color variations of the same design. What you see is basically what you get. *Camaïeu* style designs, using light and shade of one color to create a three-dimensional image, were popular in the 1950s. Painterly brush-stroke designs, mottled and shadow backgrounds, and designs in the style of famous artists were common themes. The use of gold accents elevated some fabric to designer status. Sheer lightweight silks usually presented in black worked well to bring out the beautiful colors in the florals.

5

Particularly striking are the fabrics in *Field and Garden* motif. The one-directional patterns are featured in wildflower fields or set in formal garden layout, often in bright vibrant colors. Various interpretations of the water lily are featured in *Pond Interpretations*. Several styles are shown in *Interpretations on Textured Fabrics,* many of them in ribbed weave for fall and winter. The many designs in *Leaf and Grass* range from free-form abstracts to orderly structured patterns. *Seed and Branch Patterns* highlight the popular pussywillow and windblown seed pods.

Geometric designs are divided according to motif. Many of these designs are presented in a floral motif. Some are arranged in a geometric pattern or appear with a geometric pattern background. From webs to fireworks, wild interpretations using the *Circle and Starburst* motif are fascinating examples of the creativity of the designer. The timeless polka-dot appears in various forms, particularly in fine pin-dots used as background in a design. *Plaids* and *Stripes*, too, were untraditional. *Mosaic* patterns were a popular design style. *Scrollwork* is represented in many forms, each unconventional in its own way. Different objects, from ropes to feathers, are presented in a scrollwork design.

In fabric terms, novelty designs are often called "conversational" prints. These are represented in a mixture of motifs and design styles. A sampling of

fabrics featuring *Fruit* and *Ocean* motifs is shown ranging from mosaic-style to photoprints. The designs in the *Photoprint* section will seem to jump off the page with their realistic photo images and their color intensity. Oranges are good enough to eat and the jewels ready to pin on your clothes! *Scenic Interpretations* include city and countryside images as well as wildlife vignettes. *Warp Prints,* designs created in wavy patterns, are presented in abstract geometrics and florals.

The most fascinating part of this book, however, is in the material saved for the end. These are *Special Effects* designs which are separated into four categories. Designers were intrigued with "fooling the eye", or *trompe l'oeil*, and used this medium to capture realistic images from butterflies to animal fur. Imagine wearing a fine silk fabric which looks like thick fur, or a very thin cotton which has the look of burlap.

The range of beautiful couture fabrics in this collection will delight anyone interested in French design in the 1950s. They represent many design media and motifs, and over 250 pieces of art to wear. Truly, the artist in you will be inspired.

Floral Designs
Abstract to Stylistic Interpretations

Left: Stylized "scrambled" florals, impressionistic design, low-lustre finish in rose, wine, sky blue, pale yellow, and ivory. Allover pattern. Silk. Premier season 1955.

Right: Stylized "scrambled" florals, impressionistic pattern, in wine, cobalt blue, aquamarine, cactus green, on gray brushstroke ground. Silk faille. Premier season 1955.

Top: Abstract interpretation of yellow roses. Thin polished cotton. Second season 1955.

Lower left: Abstract floral print, with a wet-wash effect. Polished cotton. Second season 1956.

Lower right: Soft tones of orange and browns in an allover floral print. Silk. Spring season 1958.

8

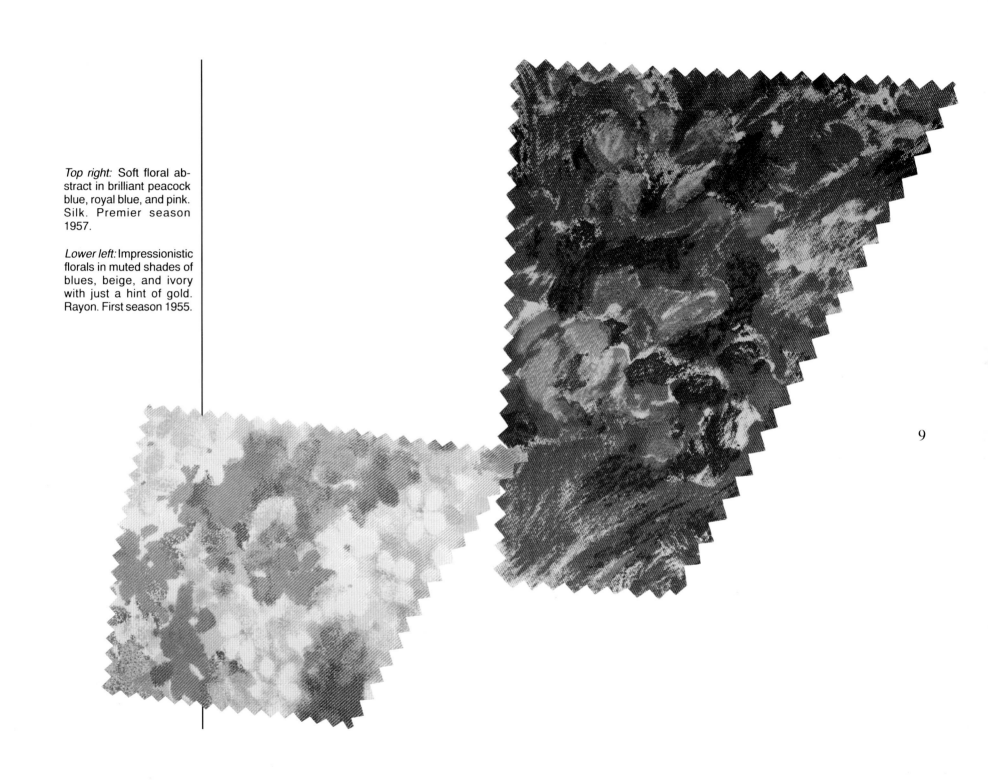

Top right: Soft floral abstract in brilliant peacock blue, royal blue, and pink. Silk. Premier season 1957.

Lower left: Impressionistic florals in muted shades of blues, beige, and ivory with just a hint of gold. Rayon. First season 1955.

9

10

Top left: The bright aqua brightens an otherwise muted floral. Rayon crêpe. First season 1956.

Top right: Abstract florals and leaves on dark cherry. Silk georgette. Second season 1955.

Lower right: Bright blue roses in a dark abstract pattern. Silk. Second season 1956.

Top right: Stylized flowers and buds on champagne ground. The bold magenta adds an unexpected splash of color to this design. Rayon. First season 1955.

Lower left: Florals and leaves with a shadow background. Semi-sheer rayon. Premier season 1957.

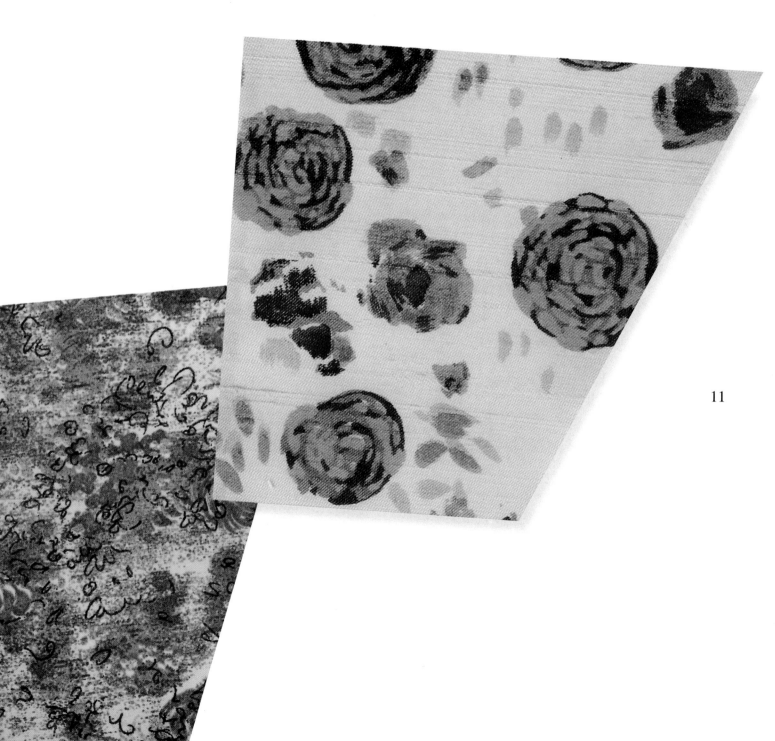

11

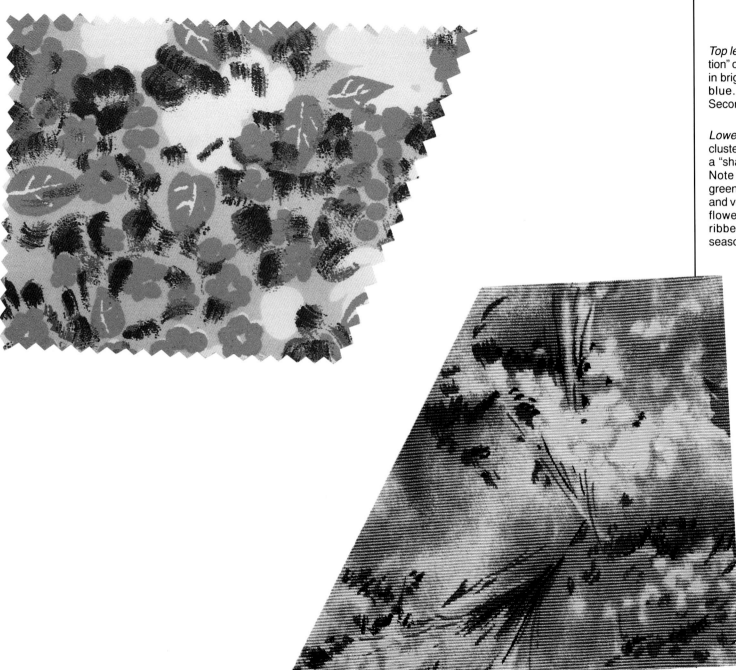

Top left: "New interpretation" of flowers and leaves in bright aquamarine and blue. Polished cotton. Second season 1955.

Lower right: Flowering clusters of branches with a "shadow" background. Note the use of forest green stems and leaves, and very pale aqua in the flower clusters. Heavy ribbed cotton. Second season 1955.

12

Top left: Magenta, pink and gold tone florals are "scrambled" in this allover packed stylized print. Rayon crêpe. First season 1955.

Top right: Stylized lilies on multicolor impressionistic ground. Numerous colors are used in the background: brown, sand, pale yellow, purple, pink, and gray. Cotton. Premier season 1955.

Lower left: Abstract floral design rendered in Van Gogh-style. Rayon and wool. Premier season 1957.

14

Top right: Stylized floral pattern executed with a finger-painting look. The color is a grayish green. Silk jersey. First season 1956.

Lower left: Broad brush strokes of color give the suggestion of a floral pattern. Bright emerald green, coral, peach, plum, yellow, aqua, dark forest green, light and medium shades of gray, and white. Cotton. Premier season 1957.

Lower right: Abstract florals in gray, dark blue, purple, and green. Cotton flannel. Winter season 1956-57.

Top right: Fluffy pompoms in this design are appropriately accompanied with the description "extremely soft-uncreasable-washable". Rayon. First season 1955.

Lower left: Heavy paint-brushed interpretation of roses, in a monotone print. Cotton. Second season 1955.

Lower right: Roses and buds in a Van Gogh-style design. Polished cotton. Second season 1956.

15

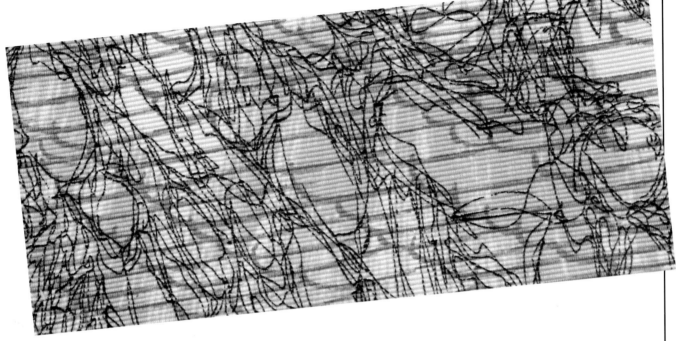

16

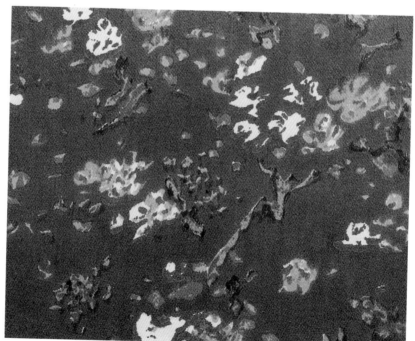

Top: Stylized line drawings of rosebuds and leaves, on sand and white ground. Note the horizon blue feather-like pattern intersecting the design. Jacquard weave effect. Cotton. Premier season 1955.

Lower: Abstract floral on medium dark khaki gray. Rayon. Second season 1956.

Left: "Jumble" pattern of turquoise, purple, and cobalt blue with scattered white roses. Cotton. Premier season 1955.

Right: Roses nestled in heavy pink and gray foliage, in an allover packed pattern. Cotton. Premier season 1955.

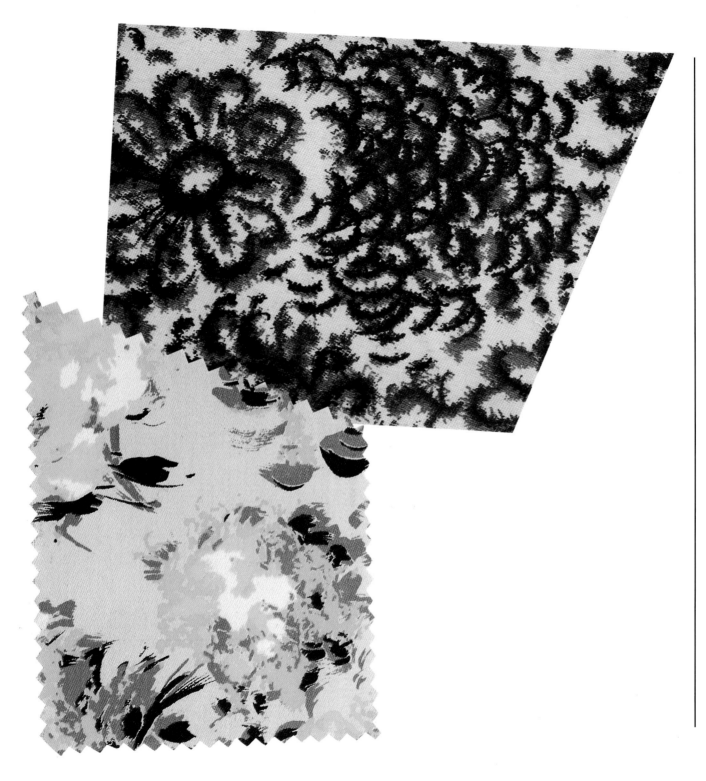

18

Top: Stylized florals and leaves in a wet-washed look, on pale yellow ground. Cotton. Second season 1955.

Lower left: Golden yellow spider mums in a stylized design, on pale aqua ground. Polished cotton. Second season 1956.

Top left: Multicolor abstract floral in peacock blue, purple, pink and gray. Rayon. Spring season 1958.

Lower right: Painterly floral abstract design in soft grays, greens and taupe. Rayon crêpe. Second season 1956.

19

Left: Dark and brilliant shades give this wildflower print a jungle feel. Rayon faille. Premier season 1957.

Top right: Subtle pink and white abstract florals are accented by dark and light gray. Cotton. Second season 1956.

Lower right: Turquoise and pink daisy floral print, with impressionistic background. Cotton. Second season 1956.

Top left: Blue daisies on mottled gray and sand ground. Cotton. Premier season 1955.

Lower right: Stylized brushstroke florals in an allover packed pattern. Cotton. Premier season 1955.

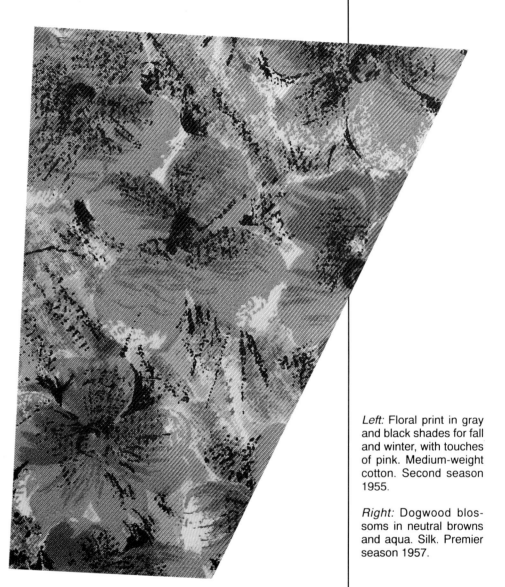

Left: Floral print in gray and black shades for fall and winter, with touches of pink. Medium-weight cotton. Second season 1955.

Right: Dogwood blossoms in neutral browns and aqua. Silk. Premier season 1957.

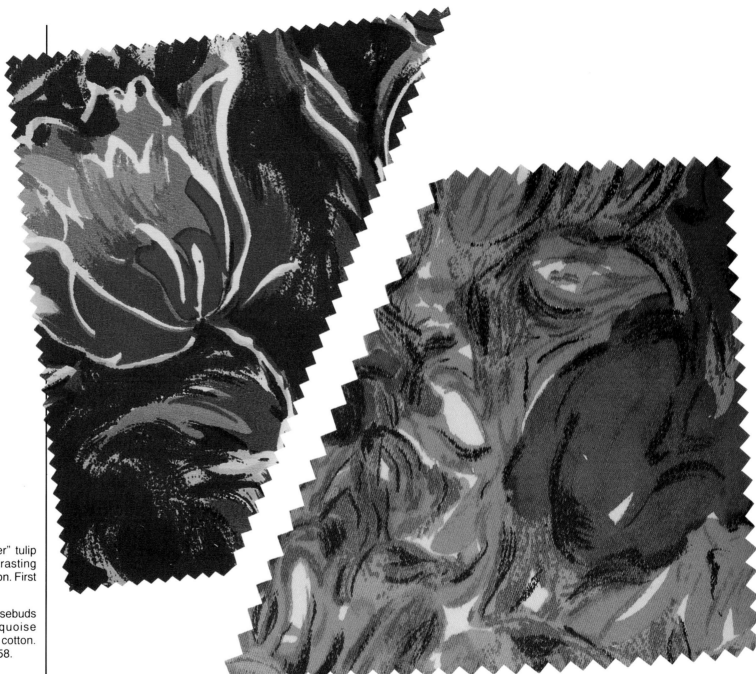

Left: "Exotic flower" tulip pattern with contrasting "hot" shades. Cotton. First season 1955.

Right: Large red rosebuds on bright turquoise ground. Polished cotton. Spring season 1958.

23

Floral Designs
Stylistic to Realistic Interpretations

Left: Stylized pink and purple florals spaced on ivory ground. Satin-backed linen. Premier season 1955.

Right: Very bright floral print in red, green, and blue. The gray flowers add dimension and fullness to the design. Polished cotton. Premier season 1957.

Top right: Romantic floral print in a soft pastel wash. Cotton. Second season 1956.

Left: Fine line drawings of floral stems on pale blue. Silk *peau de peche*. Second season 1955.

Lower right: Miniature pink carnations on dark slate blue. Silk georgette. Second season 1955.

Top left: "Oriental" look florals in neutral shades and pale lavender, with metallic gold accents. Silk crêpe de chine. Second season 1956.

Top right: Described as "modern interpretation of the flower", this swirling floral pattern is shown in peach and coral shades. Silk. First season 1955.

Lower: Pink roses and leaves on a lustrous dark gray ground. Silk crêpe de chine. Premier season 1955.

Top left: Small floral print in gold, gray, and khaki-greens on pale yellow ground. Rayon crêpe. First season 1956.

Top right: Large clusters of tiny flowers and leaves in neutral tones. Cotton chintz. First season 1955.

Lower: Delicate tiny wild-flower clusters on romantic black, with a touch of metallic gold. Very sheer cotton organdy, shown with black backing. First season 1956.

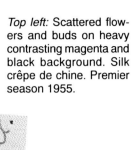

Top left: Scattered flowers and buds on heavy contrasting magenta and black background. Silk crêpe de chine. Premier season 1955.

28

Top right: One of many designs described as "new interpretations of floral bouquets", in neutral tones. Silk shantung. First season 1955.

Lower: Floral print on contrasting red and dark brown background. The bright green dots offer yet another striking contrast. Silk. Premier season 1955.

Top right: Striking gold-tone mums on solid black background. Fine silk charmeuse. Second season 1955.

Lower left: Poppies and wildflowers in yellow, cameo coral, mint green and neutral sand. The swirling grasses lend movement to the design. Cotton chintz. Second season 1956.

29

Left: Romantic print of delicate flowers on pale gray ground. Rayon. Premier season 1957.

Lower right: "New interpretation of the flower" in this tulip pattern is shown in two "new colors" for the season. Silk. First season 1956.

Top left: Blue flowers and bright pink buds stand out on a mottled, soft shadow background. Cotton. Second season 1956.

Lower: Scattered pink carnations tossed on an allover field of monotone leaves. Silk georgette. Second season 1955.

Top left: The shadowy "new interpretation of the flower" print has a dark tropical look. Silk faille. Second season 1955.

Lower left: Solid black field with tiny touches of blue and yellow florals. Cotton. Premier season 1955.

Lower right: This interpretation of a flower is a fine example of *camaïeu*, a monochrome painting using only light and shade of a single color to achieve a third dimension. The flower appears lifelike with the use of shadows. The overall pattern also shows a rose. In various shades of gray. Rayon faille. First season 1955.

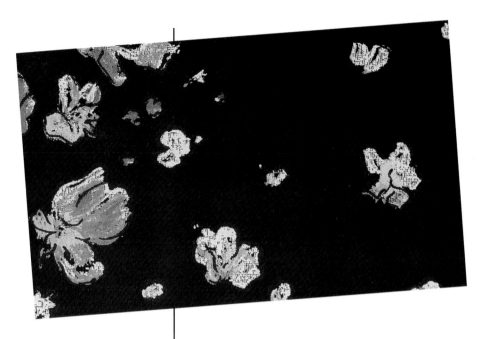

Top left: Random floating flowers and buds on black ground. Very sheer cotton organdy, shown on black backing. First season 1956.

Top right: Wildflowers and buds in finely outlined gray with touches of pink centers. This design borrows from the *idée de camaïeu.* Sheer silk georgette. Premier season 1955.

Lower left: Brilliant pink roses and buds on black. Florals in raised felt. Fabric in heavy cotton. Winter season 1956-57.

Lower right: "Romantic bouquets" on dark background. Shown over white backing. Sheer silk organdy. Second season 1956.

33

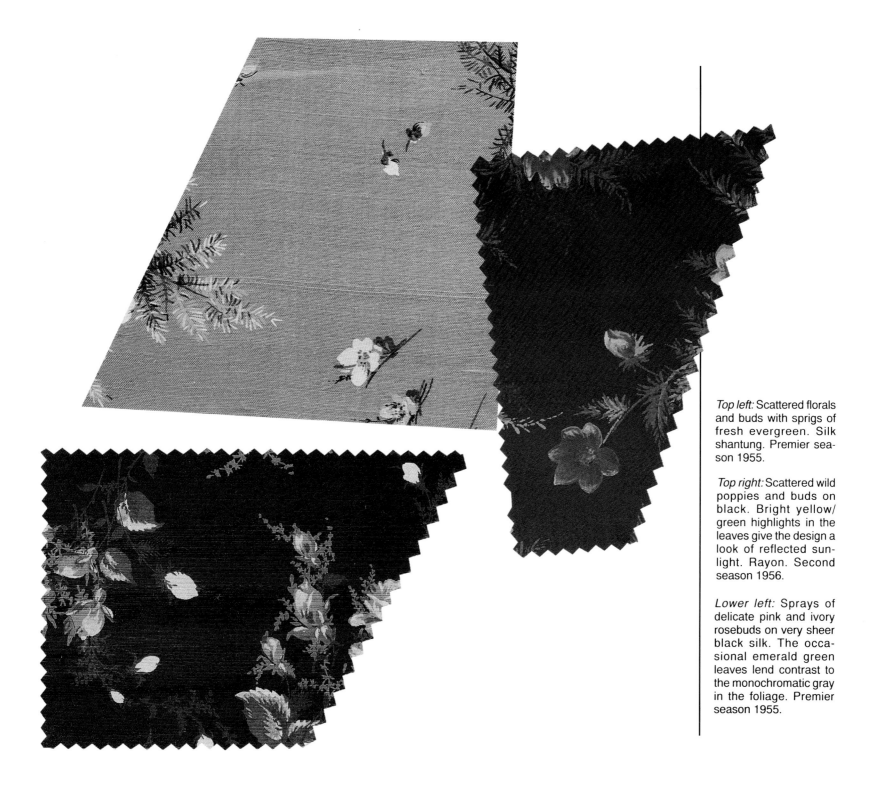

34

Top left: Scattered florals and buds with sprigs of fresh evergreen. Silk shantung. Premier season 1955.

Top right: Scattered wild poppies and buds on black. Bright yellow/ green highlights in the leaves give the design a look of reflected sunlight. Rayon. Second season 1956.

Lower left: Sprays of delicate pink and ivory rosebuds on very sheer black silk. The occasional emerald green leaves lend contrast to the monochromatic gray in the foliage. Premier season 1955.

Lower left: Extra heavy weight ribbed cotton in a floral design. Notice that thin and thick ribs alternate in the fabric. First season 1956.

Top center: Bright yellow daffodils in double-ribbed cotton velour. First season 1956.

Lower right: Blooming Christmas cacti in multi-waled cotton corduroy. First season 1956.

Floral Designs
Interpretations on Textured Fabrics

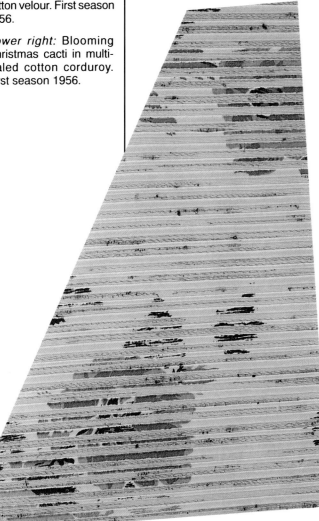

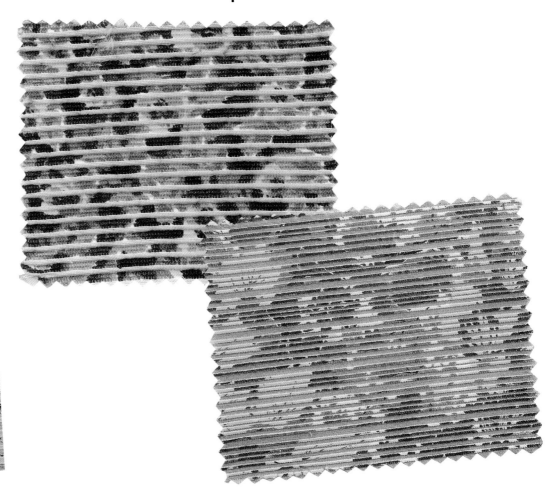

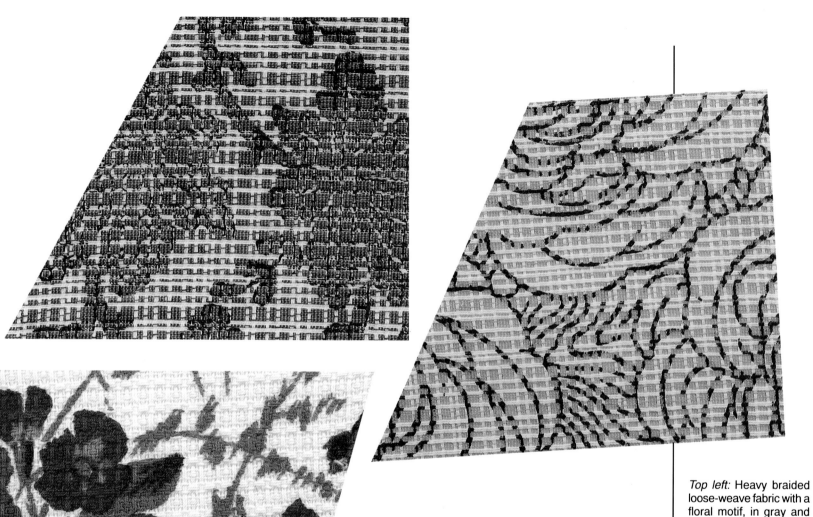

36

Top left: Heavy braided loose-weave fabric with a floral motif, in gray and black. Cotton and rayon. Premier season 1957.

Top right: Graphic line drawings of roses in a braided loose-weave fabric. Rayon and cotton. Spring season 1958.

Lower left: Bright pink and purple morning glories on white waffle weave soft cotton. Spring season 1958.

Floral Designs
Seed and Branch Patterns

Top left: Seed pods and foliage in bold maroon, browns and red, on pale yellow ground. Cotton. Second season 1956.

Lower left: Scattered tiny seeds on coral scribbled patterns. Stamped *Fond Nouveau*. Rayon. Premier season 1955.

Lower right: Seed pods in an allover pattern. Silk crêpe de chine. Second season 1955.

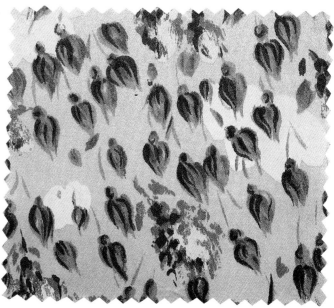

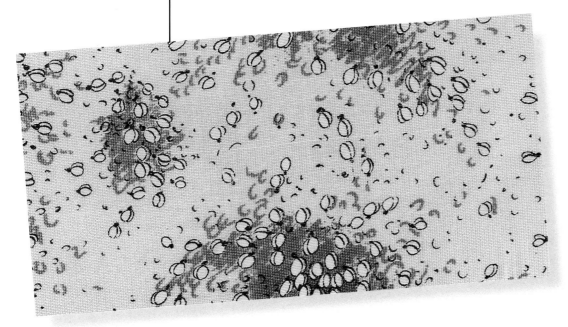

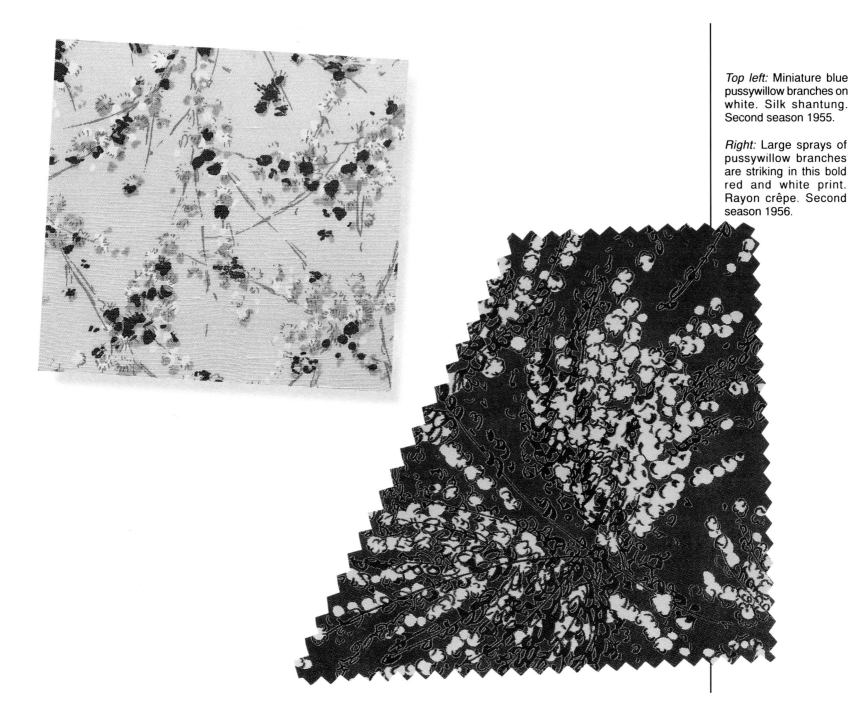

38

Top left: Miniature blue pussywillow branches on white. Silk shantung. Second season 1955.

Right: Large sprays of pussywillow branches are striking in this bold red and white print. Rayon crêpe. Second season 1956.

Floral Designs
Field and Garden Patterns

Top left: A garden of wild chrysanthemums in the colors of fall. Rayon crêpe. First season 1955.

Lower right: Anemone and aster garden in shades of magenta, gray and white on royal blue ground, in an allover packed pattern. Cotton. Premier season 1955.

40

Top left: Field of delicate poppies and wildflowers on black offers beautiful color contrasts. Cotton. Premier season 1955.

Lower right: Wildflower and grass design in shocking pink. Silk. Second season 1955.

Top left: The intensity of the black ground lends beautiful contrast to the neutral and gold tones of the floral garden. Polished cotton. Second season 1956.

Top right: Tiny clusters of flowers on gray ground. *Mousseline*, French word for muslin, is actually a very fine sheer silk in a plain weave. *Tussah* is a strong and irregular silk. Semi-sheer *mousseline tussah* silk. First season 1955.

Lower right: A bright print featuring pink and red garden primroses on black ground. Note the metallic gold touches in the green leaf branches. Allover packed design. Cotton. Premier season 1955.

41

Top: The brilliant colors in this garden pattern make a striking presentation. The fabric swatch is pinned at one end to fit into the swatch pattern book, however, the design is actually arranged in rows of a vertical stripe pattern. Polished cotton. Second season 1956.

Lower right: Garden of green bushes arranged in a diagonal pattern. Silk. Second season 1955.

42

Lower left: A garden of zinnia and asters in bright shades of blue. The pebble ground lends depth to the *camaïeu* design. Silk charmeuse. Second season 1955.

Left: Horizontal rows of flowers in a garden flower bed design. Cotton. Premier season 1955.

Right: Garden flowers in bright pink and magenta. The overall pattern displays various flowering bushes and planted florals, with each floral grouping separated by the colorful striated background. Cotton. Premier season 1955.

43

Floral Designs
Pond Interpretations

Top right: Lilies and pads in rich purple shades, crayon pastel effect. *Camaieu*-style mono-chromatic print. Multi-weave pattern. Silk. First season 1955.

Lower left: "Lake flowers" depicted in bold painterly brush strokes. Linen. First season 1955.

Lower right: Waterlilies and pads in purple, tur-quoise and blue. Rayon faille. Spring season 1958.

Top left: Monet-style pond setting with water and wild grasses. Cotton. First season 1956.

Lower right: Bright royal blue lends a striking contrast to the subtle shades of this stylized water lily print. Cotton. Second season 1956.

45

Floral Designs
Leaf and Grass Patterns

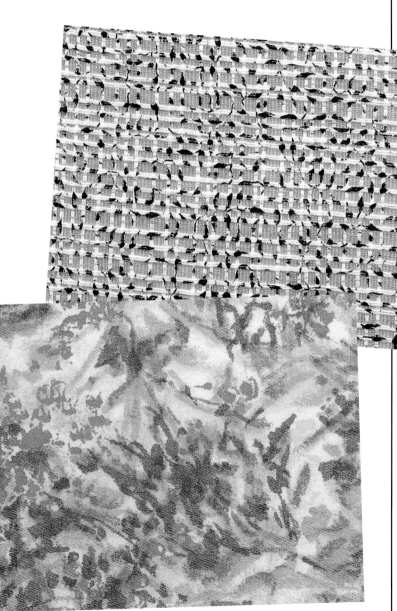

Top right: Tiny allover leaf pattern on braided loose-weave fabric. Rayon and cotton. Spring season 1958.

Lower left: This "new interpretation of leaves" is actually a design set in a larger paisley pattern. Cotton. Second season 1956.

Lower right: Watercolor effect sprigs of greenery on neutral shades. Cotton. Second season 1956.

Top left: Tiny leaves in neutral tones, allover packed pattern. Cotton. Second season 1955.

Lower left: A scattering of white and yellow flowers in dark green jungle brush ground. Cotton. Second season 1955.

Lower right: Large feathery leaves in rich brown shades. Wool flannel. Winter season 1956-57.

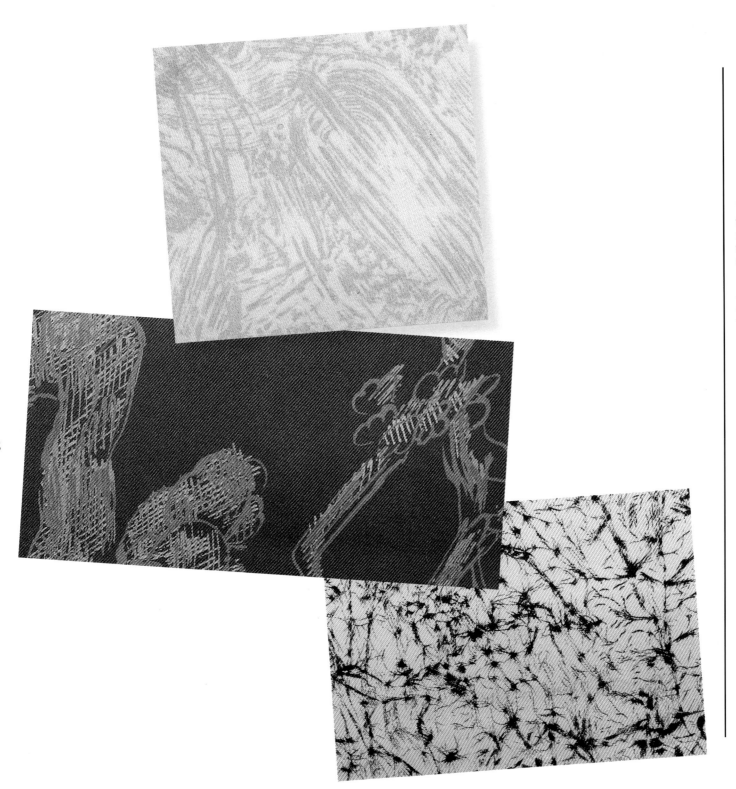

48

Top: "Imitation jacquard weave" foliage design in neutral shades. Medium-weight cotton. Second season 1955.

Center: Line drawings and cross-hatching in a stylized interpretation of florals, leaves and vines. In neutral tones on smokey gray. Silk. Second season 1955.

Lower right: A stylistic interpretation of vines and thorns on pale blue. Silk. Second season 1955.

Top left: Tossed leaves in gray, black and yellow. Cotton chintz. Second season 1955.

Top right: Very impressionistic interpretation of grasslands and florals, on dry brushed ground. Rayon crêpe. First season 1955.

Lower left: Flowering leaves and foliage in semi-sheer silk. First season 1955.

Lower right: Leaves in shades of muted pink and wine on speckled ground. Silk *peau de peche*. Second season 1955.

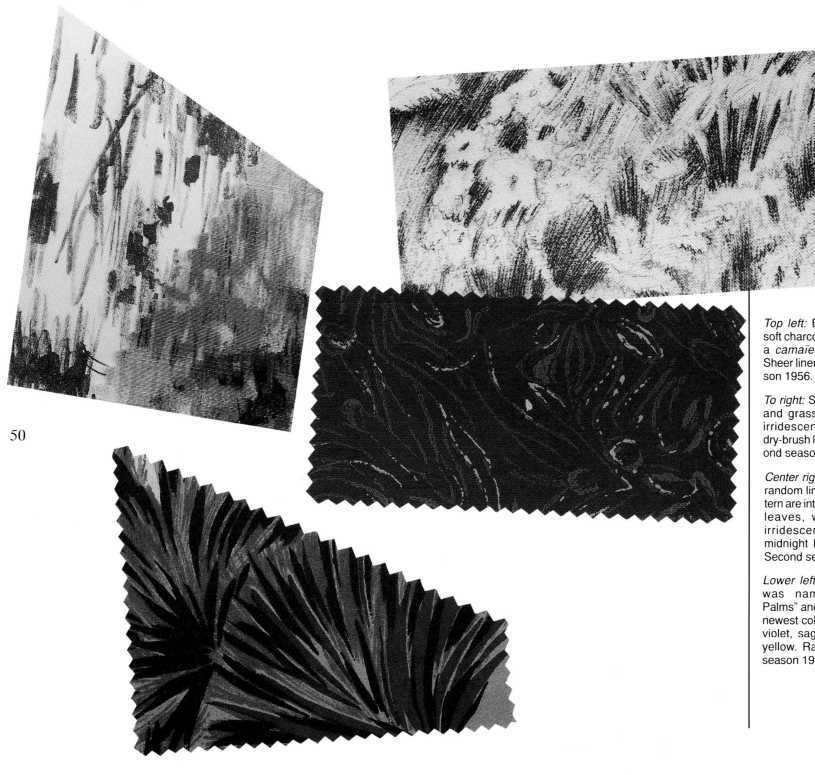

50

Top left: Branches in a soft charcoal-pencil look, a *camaïeu* effect print. Sheer linen. Second season 1956.

To right: Stylized leaves and grass in blue and irridescent white, in a dry-brush look. Silk. Second season 1955.

Center right: Seemingly random lines in this pattern are interpretations of leaves, with a slight irridescent quality. In midnight blue fine silk. Second season 1955.

Lower left: This design was named "Floral-Palms" and shown in the newest colors for spring: violet, sage green, and yellow. Rayon. Premier season 1955.

Top left: "Feather florals" in "shooting arrows" style on white ground. Again, note the use of irridescent white in the fabric design. Polished cotton. First season 1955.

Top right: This exquisite leaf and evergreen design was described as "rich impressions-washable metallic gold-on cotton." Premier season 1955.

Lower left: Wild fern on dark ground. Note the contrast of the bright pink flowers and green leaves in this design. Sheer silk organdy. Second season 1956.

Lower right: Stylized grasslands in sage green, yellow, and black. Polished cotton. Second season 1955.

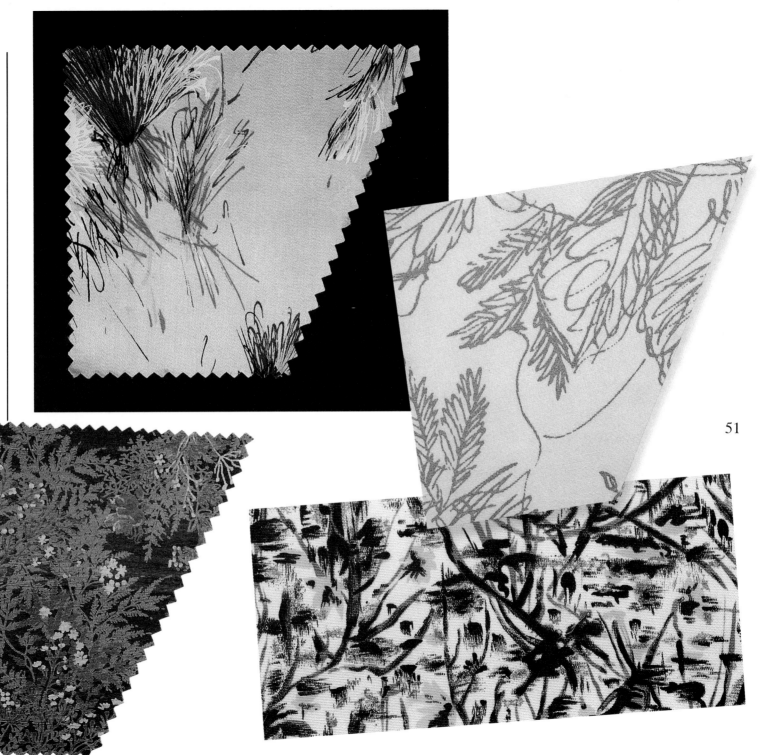

51

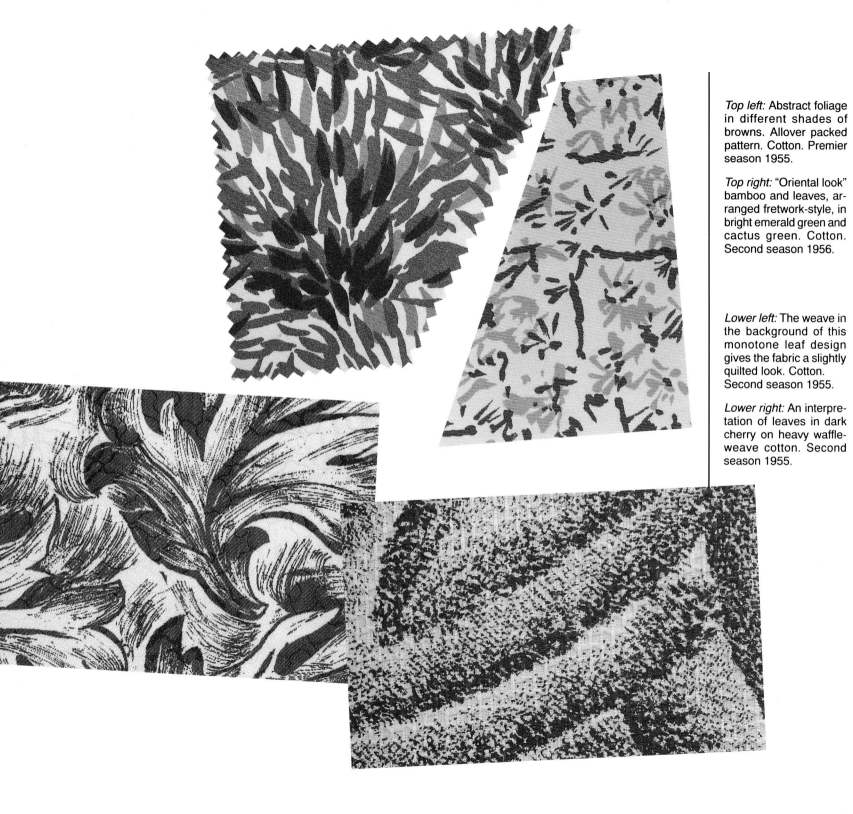

Top left: Abstract foliage in different shades of browns. Allover packed pattern. Cotton. Premier season 1955.

Top right: "Oriental look" bamboo and leaves, arranged fretwork-style, in bright emerald green and cactus green. Cotton. Second season 1956.

Lower left: The weave in the background of this monotone leaf design gives the fabric a slightly quilted look. Cotton. Second season 1955.

Lower right: An interpretation of leaves in dark cherry on heavy waffle-weave cotton. Second season 1955.

Geometric Designs
Stripe Patterns

Left: Op-art look design with colorful geometric boxes, on irregular striped ground. Very thin ribbed cotton. First season 1955.

Right: Feather-edged gray and white stripe pattern. Satin-backed cotton. Premier season 1957.

54

Top: Delicate pink and white stripes with small roses woven in for textural interest. The stripes are subtle background to the fruit motif. Stamped *Fond Nouveau.* Cotton. Premier season 1955.

Center right: Scattered rosebuds on a streaked background, in "modern colors" of purple, and bright orange. Rayon. First season 1955.

Lower left: Described as a "new interpretation of a flower", this monochromatic floral print is crossed with bold vertical stripes. Rayon. First season 1955.

Top: This interesting fabric in ribbed *pékin* stripes features very bright colors in a stylized floral pattern, with a shadow effect between colors. *Pékin* is a textile with equal width stripes and spaces between the stripes. It is usually used in novelty fabrics with other fibers, in this case, with mousseline silk. Very sheer *mousseline pékin* silk. First season 1955.

Lower left: Gray and white stripes, edged with tiny black and white dots. Cotton. Premier season 1957.

Lower right: Tiny columns of pastel flowers in black and white hatband stripes. Cotton. First season 1956.

56

Top left: "Persian style" floral frames on gray striped silk organdy and black striped satin. Very sheer, shown over white background. Second season 1956.

Lower right: Same design and fabric shown over black background.

Geometric Designs
Checks and Plaid Patterns

Top left: This novelty plaid design has the look of set-in gemstones. Polished cotton. Second season 1956.

Top right: Houndstooth pattern in textured cross-rib weave. Rayon and cotton. Spring season 1958.

Lower: Tiny black and white checks lend beautiful contrast to the pink roses. Part of the fabric swatch is pinned back to show the diagonal rose pattern in the overall design. Rayon crêpe. First season 1955.

58

Top left: Loud cross-grids in a "diamond" pattern, described as a "country sport" design. Semi-stiff linen. First season 1955.

Lower left: Stylized florals in geometric fretwork pattern. Rayon. First season 1956.

Lower right: Roses spaced on bright orange ground, accented with metallic gold stripes in a modified basketweave pattern. Cotton. Spring season 1958.

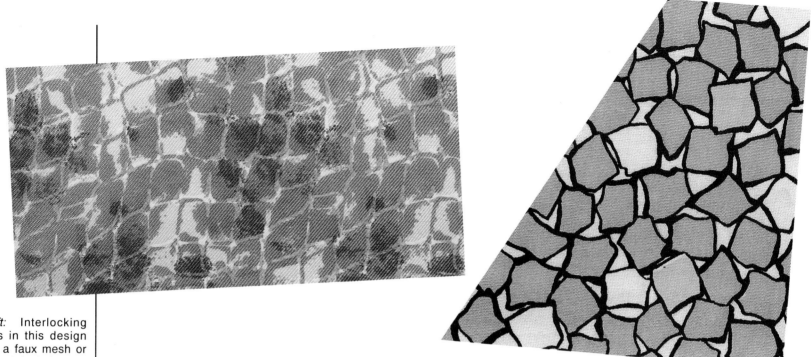

Top left: Interlocking squares in this design gives it a faux mesh or honeycomb look. In neutral browns and beige. Rayon. First season 1955.

Top right: Geometric shapes in beige and white, arranged mosaic-style. Randomly placed aqua color adds interest to the design. Cotton. First season 1955.

Lower left: Butterflies are shown behind a lattice pattern rope fence in this *trompe l'oeil* print. The shadow image behind the fencing gives the design a three-dimensional look. Cotton chintz. Second season 1956.

Lower right: Floral motif in a geometric diamond pattern. Cotton. First season 1956.

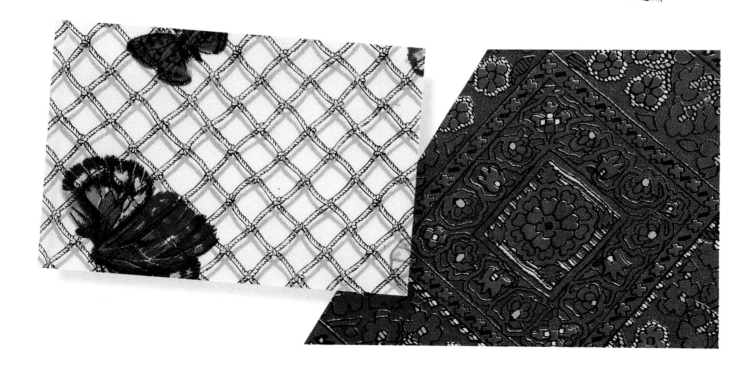

Geometric Designs
Dot Patterns

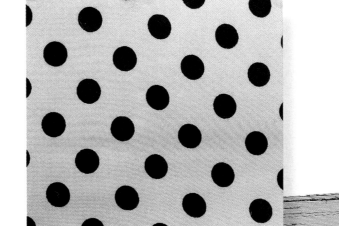

Top center: Navy polka dots on white satin. First season 1955.

Center right: Red dots on a striated champagne ground. Sheer silk georgette. First season 1955.

Lower left: Vibrant red and pink rosebuds stand out in an emerald green pin-dot ground. The shadow effect under each bud gives this pattern a three-dimensional look. Silk shantung. First season 1955.

Top left: A raised woven windowpane check and tiny pin dots provide an interesting background to this pansy print. Linen. Premier season 1955.

Top right: Circular patches of a stylized vine design are spaced on pin-dot ground. Metallic gold on white. Polished cotton. First season 1956.

Lower left: Dark brown "polka dots and lozenges", on heavy corded-effect woven cotton. First season 1955.

Lower right: Large leaf with a watercolor wash-look shadow, polka-dots on pink champagne ground. The overall design of this fabric alternates small and large leaves. Cotton chintz. First season 1955.

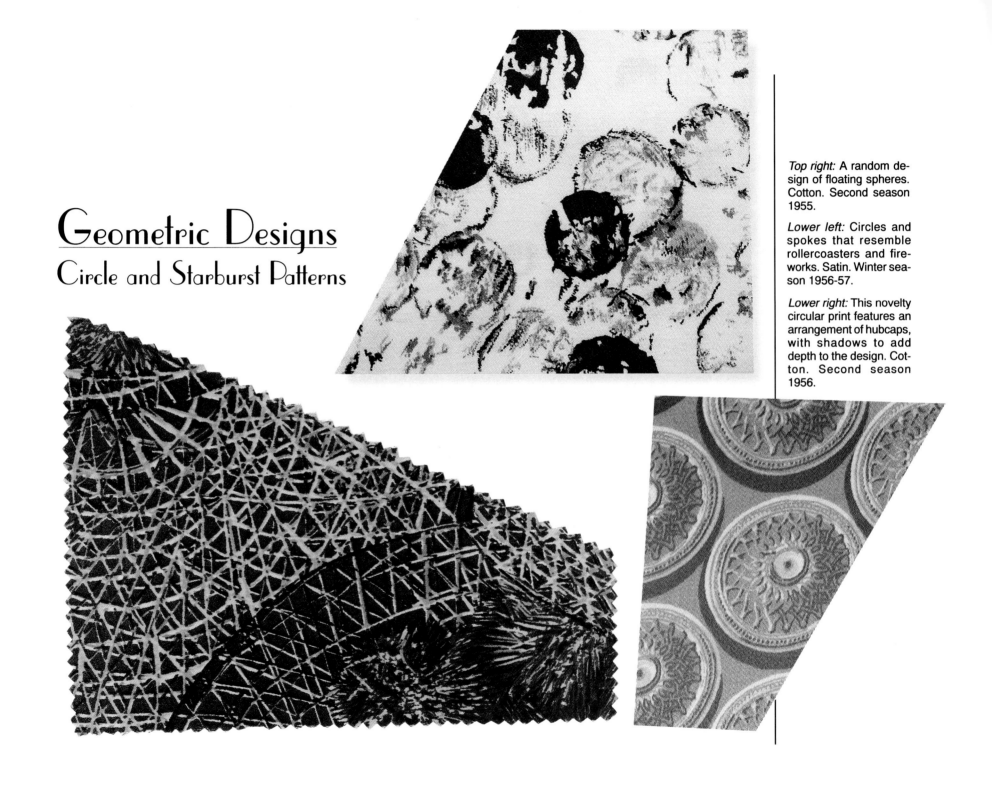

Geometric Designs
Circle and Starburst Patterns

Top right: A random design of floating spheres. Cotton. Second season 1955.

Lower left: Circles and spokes that resemble rollercoasters and fireworks. Satin. Winter season 1956-57.

Lower right: This novelty circular print features an arrangement of hubcaps, with shadows to add depth to the design. Cotton. Second season 1956.

Top left: Large snowflake patterns on bright red background. Heavy felt. Winter season 1956-67.

Top right: Ruffled starbursts on speckled yellow ground. Silk crêpe de chine. First season 1956.

Lower left: large circular web pattern on bright turquoise background. Silk. Spring season 1958.

63

64

Left: Shades of magenta and purple explode in a festive floral starburst pattern. Cotton. Premier season 1955.

Right: Wild splashes of multicolor florals in a starburst pattern. Cotton. Premier season 1955.

Geometric Designs
Loops and Scrollwork

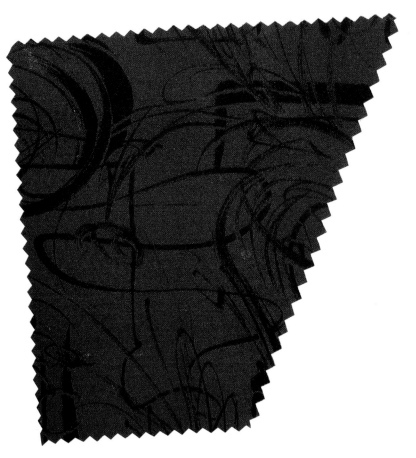

Left: Garlands of florals intertwine with feathery scrolling leaves. Rayon. First season 1955.

Right: Loops and swirls in abstract brush strokes, rich red background. Heavy cotton. Winter season 1956-57.

66

Top right: Feathery *fleur-de-lis* on tiny striated shadow background, with metallic gold trim. Cotton. Second season 1956.

Lower left: Floral cartouches framed by rope curves. This design has a mosaic look. Cotton. Second season 1955.

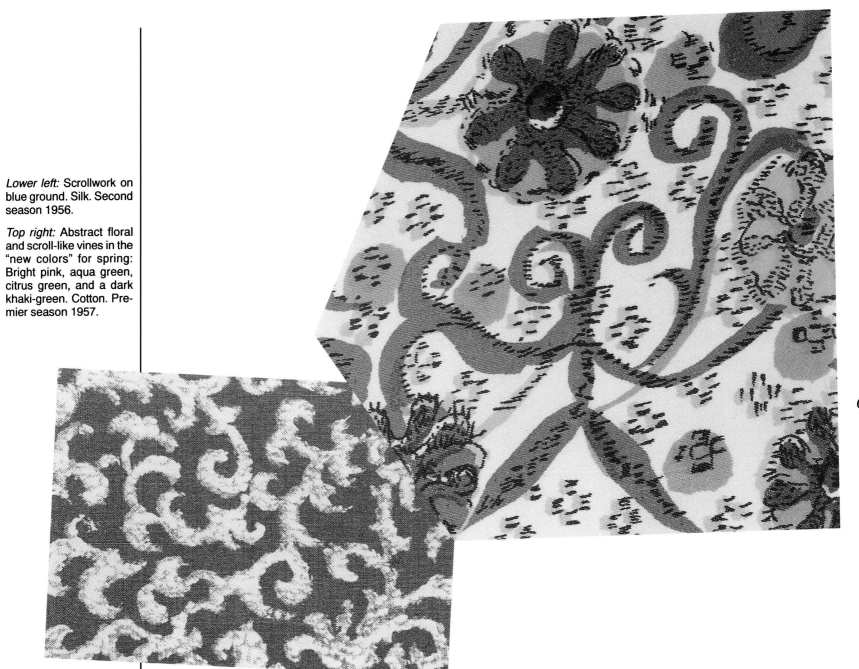

Lower left: Scrollwork on blue ground. Silk. Second season 1956.

Top right: Abstract floral and scroll-like vines in the "new colors" for spring: Bright pink, aqua green, citrus green, and a dark khaki-green. Cotton. Premier season 1957.

67

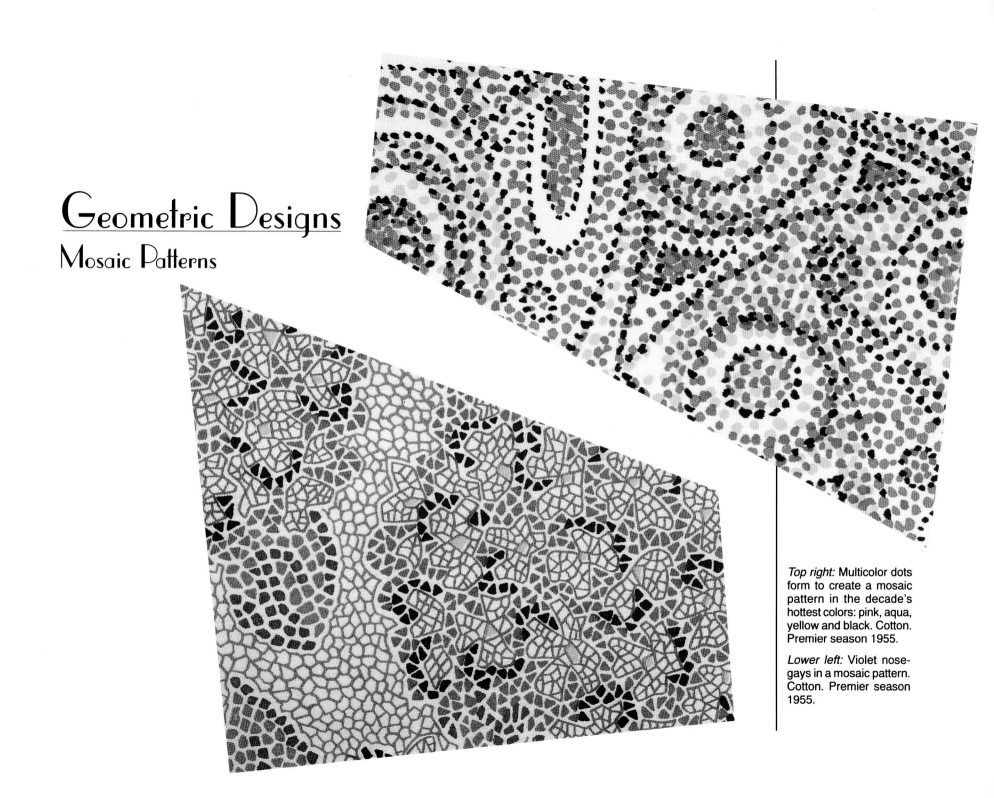

Geometric Designs
Mosaic Patterns

Top right: Multicolor dots form to create a mosaic pattern in the decade's hottest colors: pink, aqua, yellow and black. Cotton. Premier season 1955.

Lower left: Violet nose-gays in a mosaic pattern. Cotton. Premier season 1955.

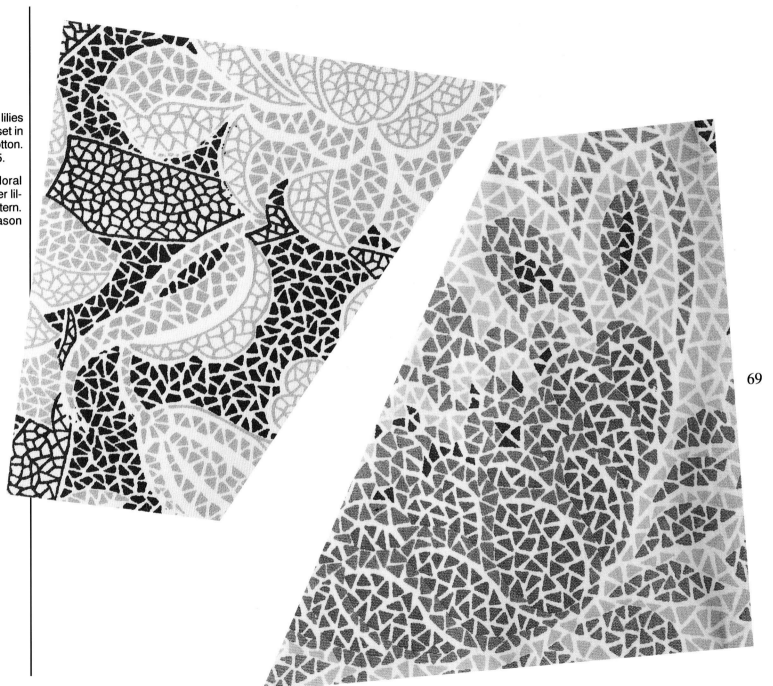

Top left: Aqua water lilies in a navy blue pond, set in a mosaic pattern. Cotton. Premier season 1955.

Lower right: "New floral interpretation" of water lilies set in a mosaic pattern. Cotton. Premier season 1955.

69

Geometric Designs
Paisley Patterns

Top three swatches: Tiny paisley pattern in three shades with diagonal ribbed weave. Silk. Second season 1956.

Lower right: This pattern features a paisley border printed on extra soft and extra wide-wale cotton chenille. Note the basket-weave effect on each rib. First season 1956.

Top right: Poppies and feathery paisley shapes, on pale aqua ground. Sheer silk georgette. Second season 1956.

Lower left: Heavy braided loose-weave fabric with a floral paisley motif, in pink and black. Cotton and rayon. Premier season 1957.

Lower right: Paisley and pin-dots on heavy unbleached linen. Second season 1956.

71

Geometric Designs
Abstracts Patterns

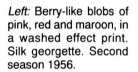

Left: Berry-like blobs of pink, red and maroon, in a washed effect print. Silk georgette. Second season 1956.

Right: Swirling gouache effect pattern, multicolor includes black, aqua, rose pink, coral pink, oxide red, and white on French gray ground. Silk. Premier season 1955.

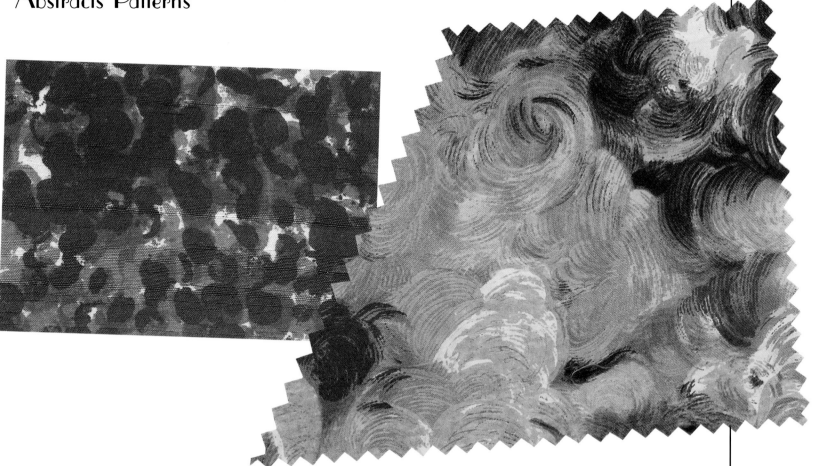

Top left: This design was named "dancing shadows". Again, the use of an unexpected splash of aqua gives the pattern interest. Silk. First season 1955.

Lower right: The shocking bold orange in this wild pattern is appropriately named "crazy wind". Linen. First season 1955.

74

Top left: Small feathery strokes in muted shades of gray, sand, and lilac arranged in semi-circular links. Cotton. First season 1955.

Lower right: Multicolor molecular shapes float on gray ground. Cotton. Premier season 1957.

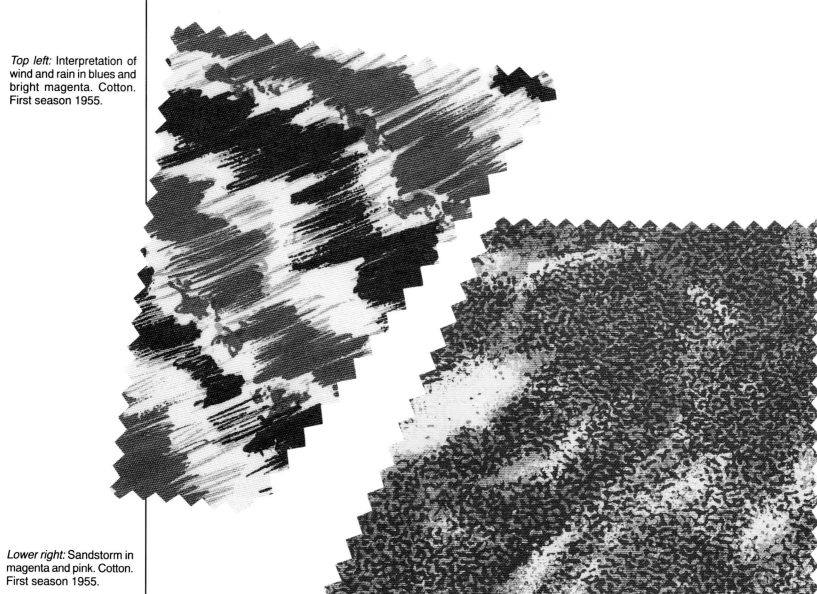

Top left: Interpretation of wind and rain in blues and bright magenta. Cotton. First season 1955.

Lower right: Sandstorm in magenta and pink. Cotton. First season 1955.

76

Fiery flames of bright red, orange and yellow, in an impressionistic interpretation of florals. Cotton. Spring season 1958.

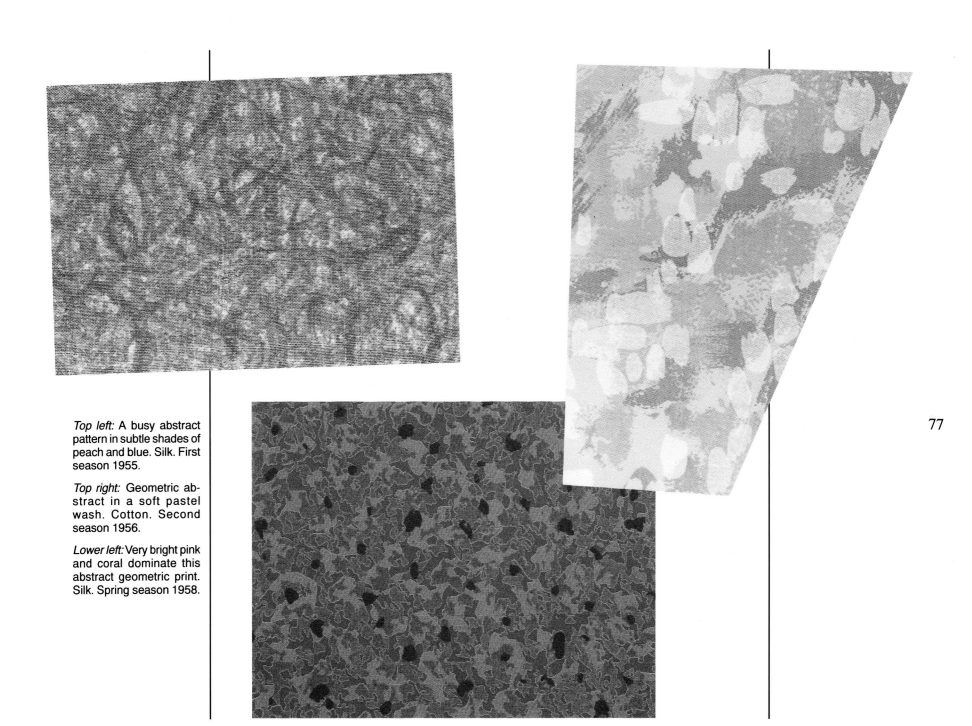

Top left: A busy abstract pattern in subtle shades of peach and blue. Silk. First season 1955.

Top right: Geometric abstract in a soft pastel wash. Cotton. Second season 1956.

Lower left: Very bright pink and coral dominate this abstract geometric print. Silk. Spring season 1958.

Top left: Geometric all-over pattern in greens and yellow, accented by black. Rayon. First season 1955.

Lower right: Cross-hatch dry brush design in blues and aquas, with random touches of bright yellow. Cotton. First season 1955.

78

79

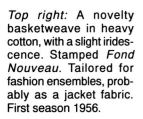

Top right: A novelty basketweave in heavy cotton, with a slight iridescence. Stamped *Fond Nouveau.* Tailored for fashion ensembles, probably as a jacket fabric. First season 1956.

Lower left: Drops of bright cherry pink and brick red in a watercolor vertical splatter pattern. Rayon crêpe. Spring season 1958.

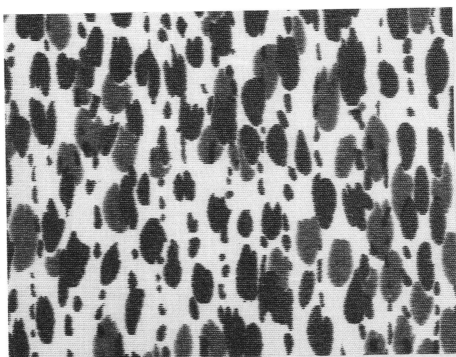

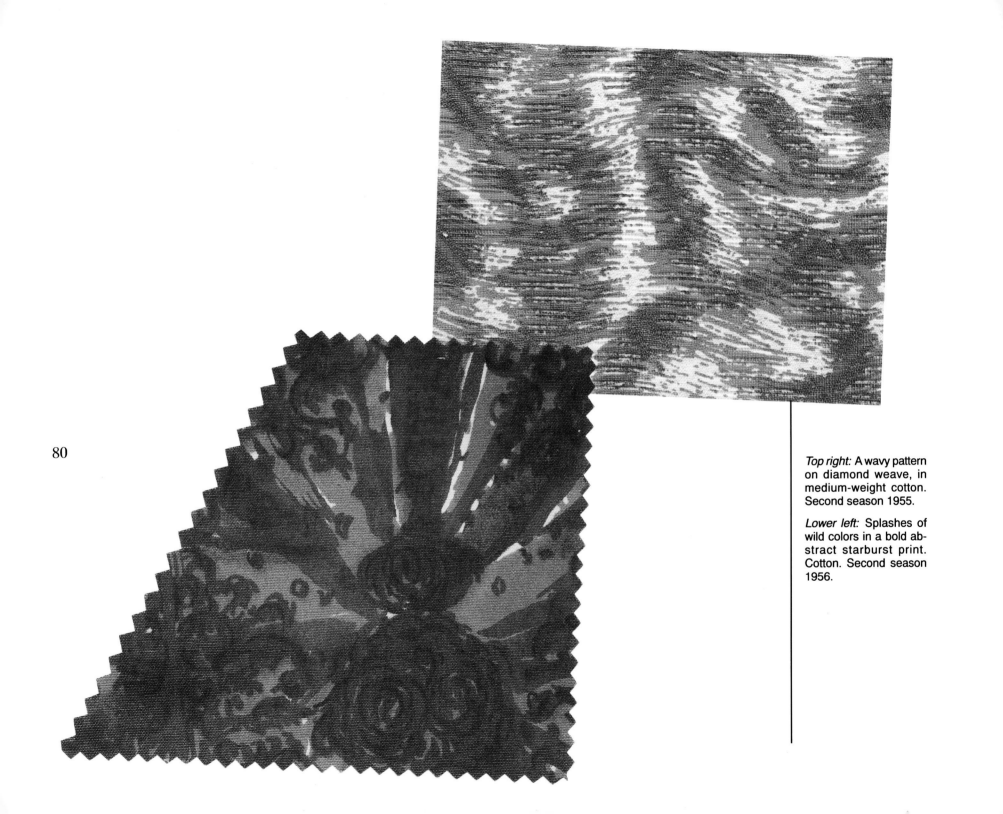

80

Top right: A wavy pattern on diamond weave, in medium-weight cotton. Second season 1955.

Lower left: Splashes of wild colors in a bold abstract starburst print. Cotton. Second season 1956.

Left: Spaced bright berries on an allover leaf pattern. Neutral shade on black ground. Silk. First season 1956.

Right: Bright red berry on white. The use of shadows was a popular design trend, and add to the *trompe l'oeil* effect. Cotton. Premier season 1955.

Novelty Designs
Fruit Patterns

Top left: Interpretation of cherries, with stems arranged in a scrollwork motif. Rayon crêpe. Premier season 1957.

Lower right: Strawberries in a field of dark blue leaves. Silk. Second season 1956.

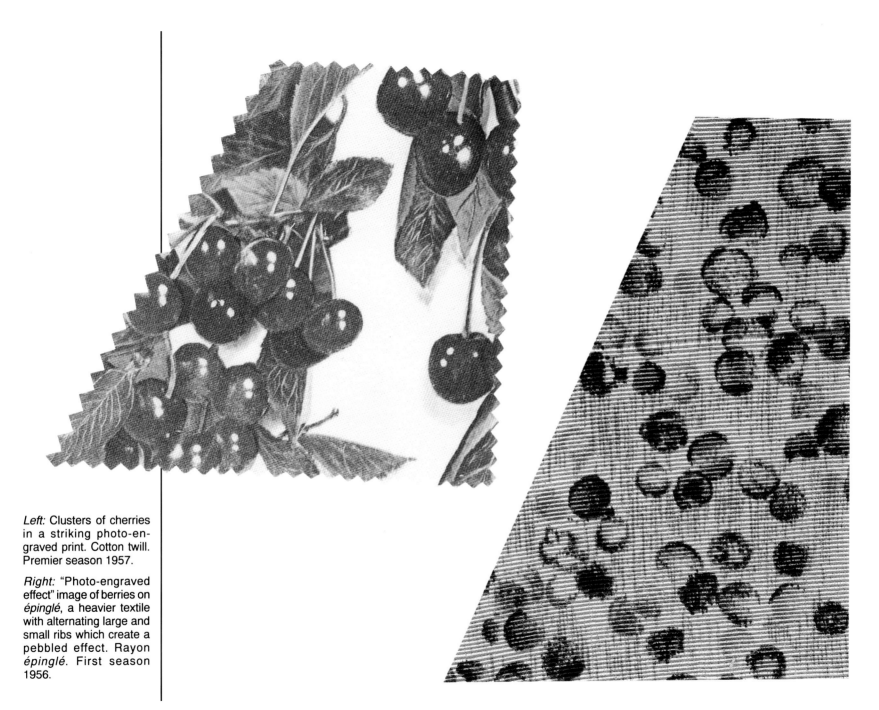

Left: Clusters of cherries in a striking photo-engraved print. Cotton twill. Premier season 1957.

Right: "Photo-engraved effect" image of berries on *épinglé*, a heavier textile with alternating large and small ribs which create a pebbled effect. Rayon *épinglé*. First season 1956.

83

Top left: Stylized impression of fruit, including pineapple and strawberries in shades of brown, beige, mint green, and bold cobalt blue. Linen. First season 1955.

Lower right: "Exotic Fruits" pattern with large pineapples. Cotton. First season 1955.

84

Novelty Designs
Ocean Patterns

Top: Large sea shells in blues and sand. Cotton. First season 1955.

Lower left: Ocean coral in shades of gray and black, printed on ivory background. Cotton grosgrain. First season 1955.

Lower right: Shells on a pebble beach. Cotton. First season 1955.

Novelty Designs

Scenic Interpretations

Previous page: Ancient Roman castles and countryside scenes. Soft cotton flannel. Winter season 1956-57.

This page, top left: Rooftop view of a city scene in black and white with touches of metallic gold. Cotton. Second season 1955.

This page, lower right: Photo-engraved images of city skyscrapers, bridges and landmarks superimposed on a faux woven background. Silk charmeuse. Second season 1955.

87

88

Top left: Monochromatic design with a loosely woven look. Cotton. Premier season 1955.

Lower: Impressionistic interpretation of a topographical desert-like landscape, in gray, black, and champagne. Note the use of picotage, or "pinning" to add texture. Rayon crêpe. First season 1955.

Opposite page, center left: Tapestry weave style fabric with images of wheatstalks, bridges, and huts, aqua on white ground. The faint gray images visible under the white are not part of the design, but rather, the design sketch shown through the thin fabric. Cotton. First season 1955.

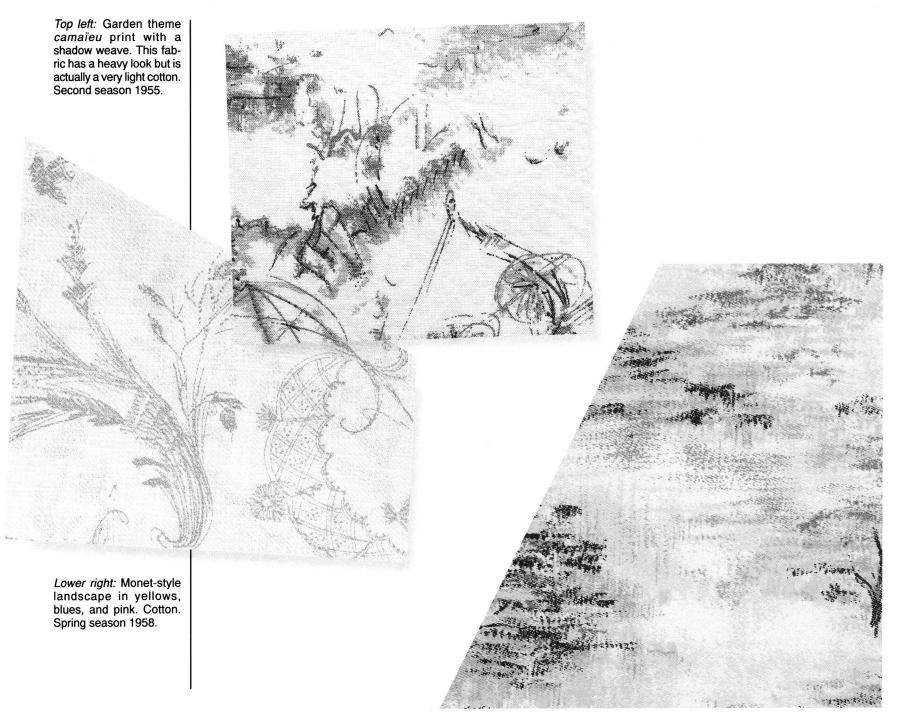

Top left: Garden theme *camaïeu* print with a shadow weave. This fabric has a heavy look but is actually a very light cotton. Second season 1955.

Lower right: Monet-style landscape in yellows, blues, and pink. Cotton. Spring season 1958.

90

Top left: Wildlife vignettes in magenta. This design is in the likeness of the classic scenic fabrics of Jouy, France, which use etched copper plates to print in a single color. Rayon. Premier season 1955.

Lower right: Stylized birds, muted plum on ivory ground. Polished cotton. First season 1955.

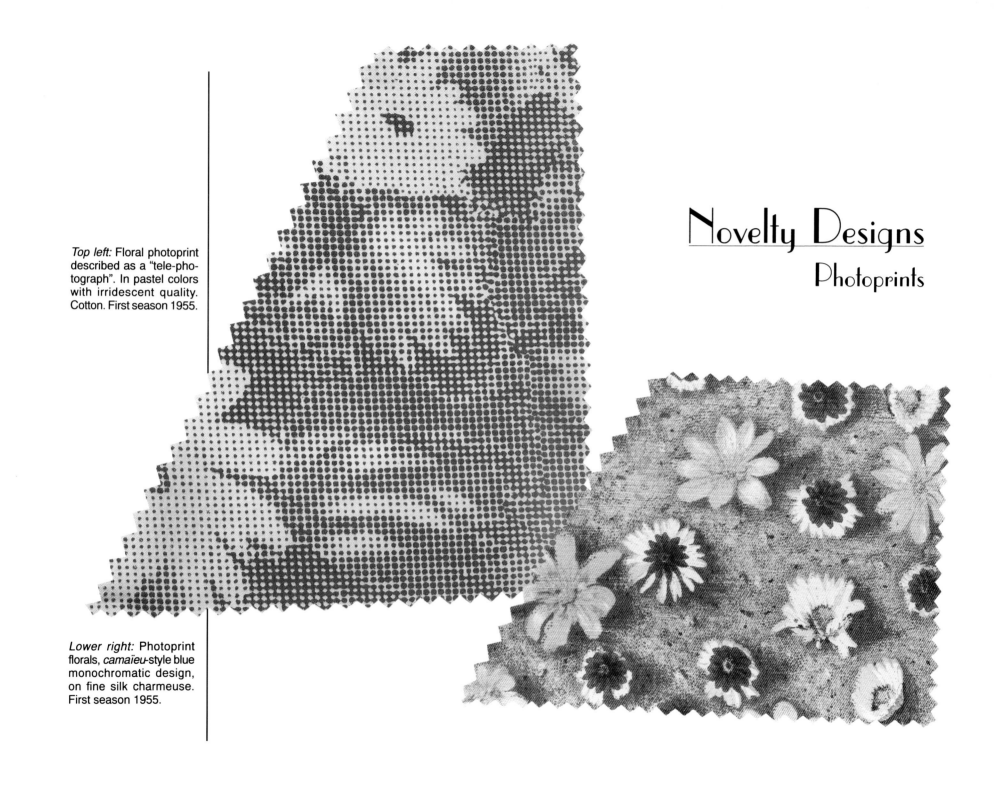

Novelty Designs
Photoprints

Top left: Floral photoprint described as a "tele-photograph". In pastel colors with irridescent quality. Cotton. First season 1955.

Lower right: Photoprint florals, *camaïeu*-style blue monochromatic design, on fine silk charmeuse. First season 1955.

92

Photo-engraved image of brilliant gemstones on woven ground. Rayon. First season 1956.

Photo-engraved image of fruits and vegetables on gravel ground. Polished cotton. First season 1956.

93

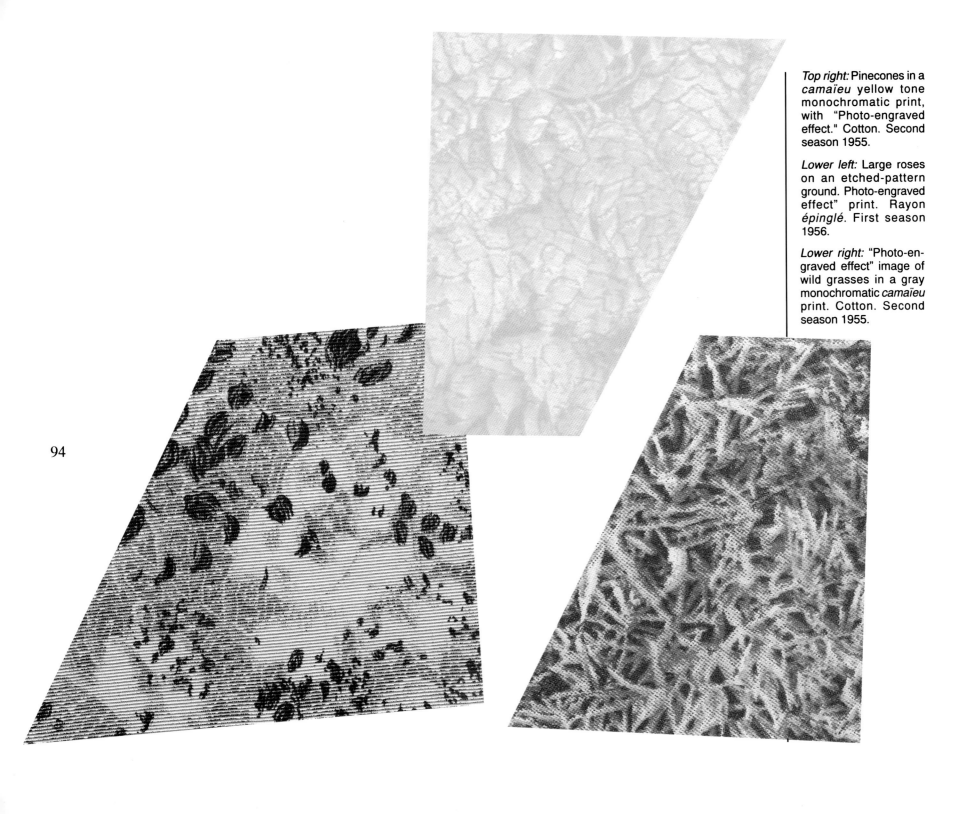

94

Top right: Pinecones in a *camaïeu* yellow tone monochromatic print, with "Photo-engraved effect." Cotton. Second season 1955.

Lower left: Large roses on an etched-pattern ground. Photo-engraved effect" print. Rayon *épinglé.* First season 1956.

Lower right: "Photo-engraved effect" image of wild grasses in a gray monochromatic *camaïeu* print. Cotton. Second season 1955.

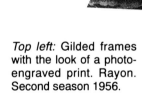

Top left: Gilded frames with the look of a photo-engraved print. Rayon. Second season 1956.

Lower right: Blooming cacti in a photo-engraved print. Polished cotton. First season 1956.

95

Novelty Designs
Warp Prints

Top right: Warp prints feature wavy instead of straight lines to form shapes. This satin-look abstract design is in muti-shades of neutral tones. Cotton chintz. Premier season 1955.

Center right: Geometric warp print in gray, bronze, black and blue. Cotton. Premier season 1955.

Lower left: Colorful impressionistic warp print with a watercolor effect. The overall design features floral bouquets. Cotton. Premier season 1955.

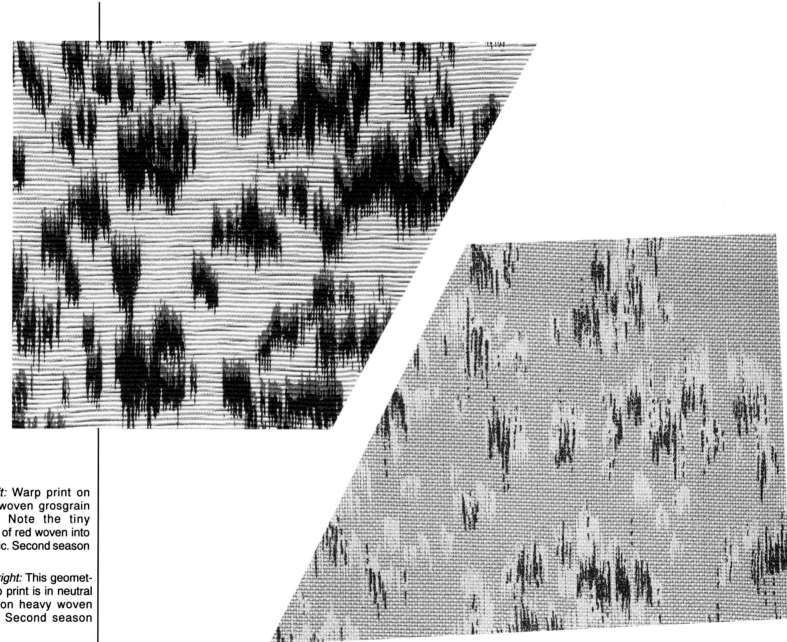

Top left: Warp print on heavy woven grosgrain cotton. Note the tiny threads of red woven into the fabric. Second season 1955.

Lower right: This geometric warp print is in neutral colors on heavy woven cotton. Second season 1955.

Novelty Designs
Special Effects - Needlework

Lower left: Multicolor yarns in a heavy stitchery pattern. Note the use of a diagonal weave over a horizontal stripe pattern. Rayon faille. Premier season 1955.

Top right: Tiny hearts fill this tapestry-look print in bright aqua, black and white. Linen. Spring season 1958.

Top left: Trompe l'oeil floral crewel-embroidery in browns, reds and greens. Cotton. Spring season 1958.

Lower left: Trompe l'oeil crewel-embroidery, on bright royal blue ground. Cotton. Spring season 1958.

Lower right: Trompe l'oeil crewel-embroidery, in multi-shades of green. Cotton. Spring season 1958.

99

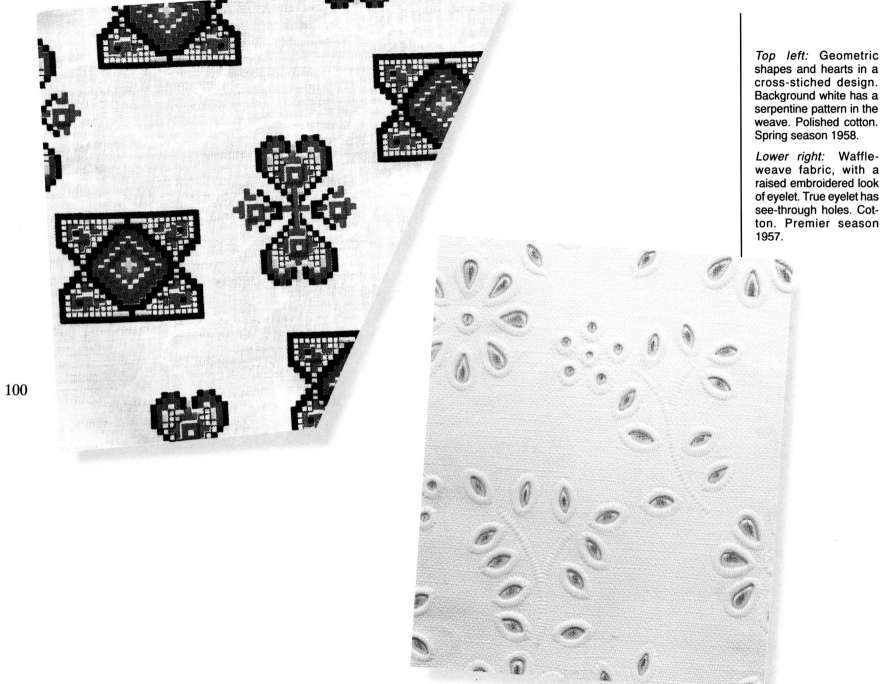

100

Top left: Geometric shapes and hearts in a cross-stiched design. Background white has a serpentine pattern in the weave. Polished cotton. Spring season 1958.

Lower right: Waffle-weave fabric, with a raised embroidered look of eyelet. True eyelet has see-through holes. Cotton. Premier season 1957.

"Pillow lace" relief design
in very fine silk. Second
season 1955.

Novelty Designs
Special Effects - Weave

Lower left: Woven effect design in gray, champagne, and blue, with scattered splotches of black. Note the etched butterfly-like designs throughout the pattern. Rayon. Premier season 1955.

Lower left: Textured weave in rich dark browns. Linen. Winter season 1956-57.

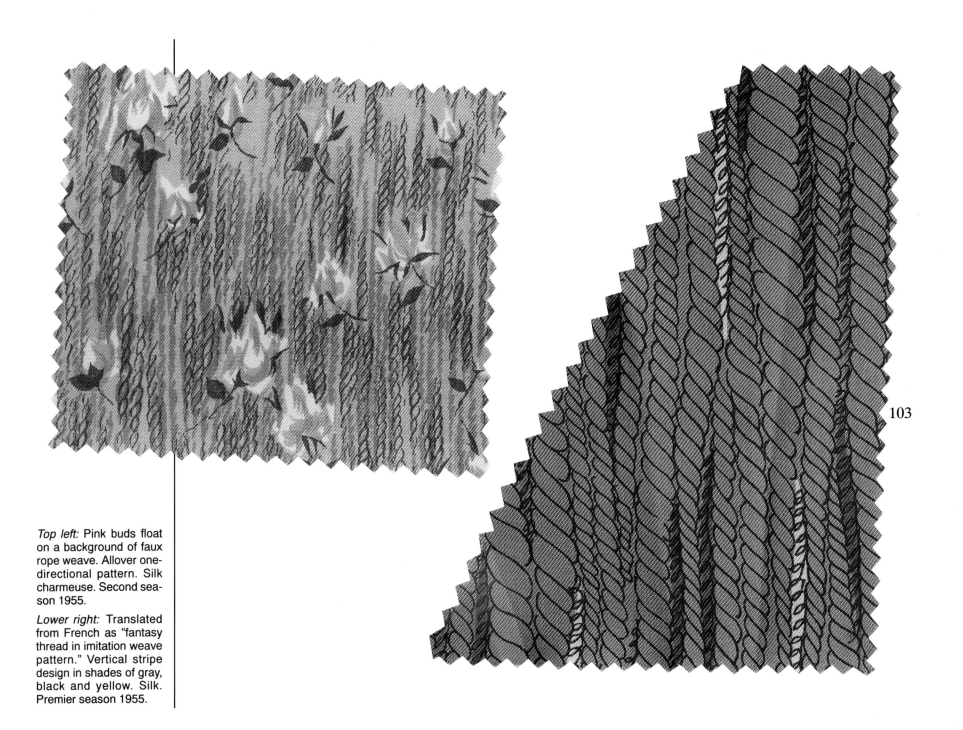

Top left: Pink buds float on a background of faux rope weave. Allover one-directional pattern. Silk charmeuse. Second season 1955.

Lower right: Translated from French as "fantasy thread in imitation weave pattern." Vertical stripe design in shades of gray, black and yellow. Silk. Premier season 1955.

103

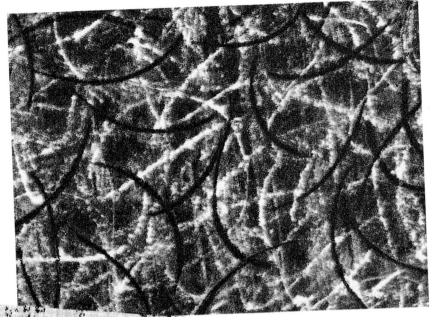

104

Top: Black and white strokes on this design create a textured napped look. Polished cotton. Second season 1955.

Lower: A floral design in an imitation lacy-weave pattern. In neutral tones and black. Cotton. First season 1956.

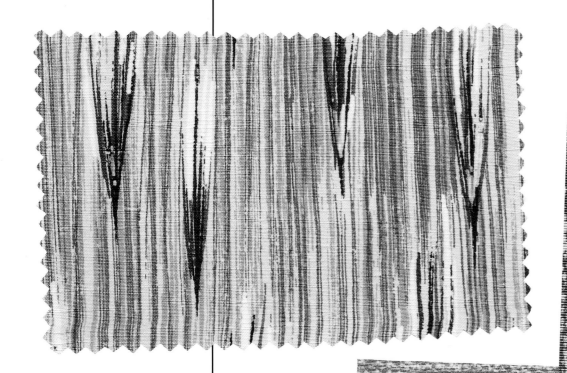

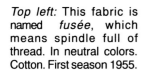

Top left: This fabric is named *fusée*, which means spindle full of thread. In neutral colors. Cotton. First season 1955.

Top right: Imitation weave in red and ivory. Rayon crêpe. First season 1955.

Lower left: Imitation burlap on very thin cotton. Second season 1955.

105

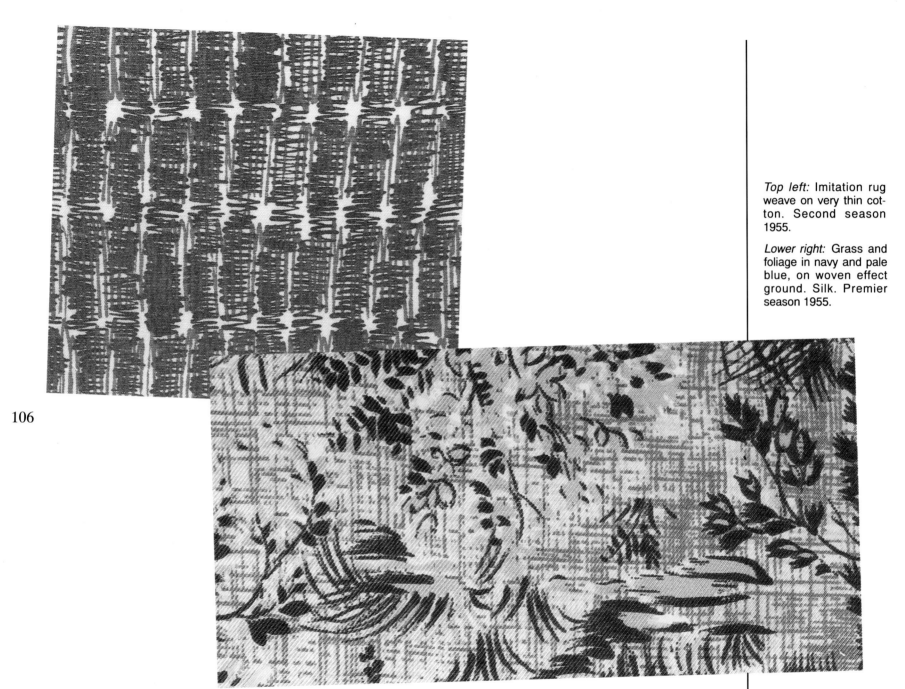

Top left: Imitation rug weave on very thin cotton. Second season 1955.

Lower right: Grass and foliage in navy and pale blue, on woven effect ground. Silk. Premier season 1955.

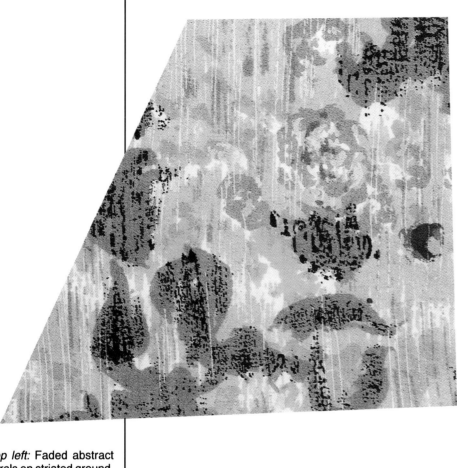

Top left: Faded abstract florals on striated ground, with a textured look. Very thin cotton. Second season 1955.

Lower right: Semi-sheer floral pattern in black, irridescent white and ivory. This fabric, though sheer, has a rigid, coarse feel and a slight shine. Silk organza. Second season 1955.

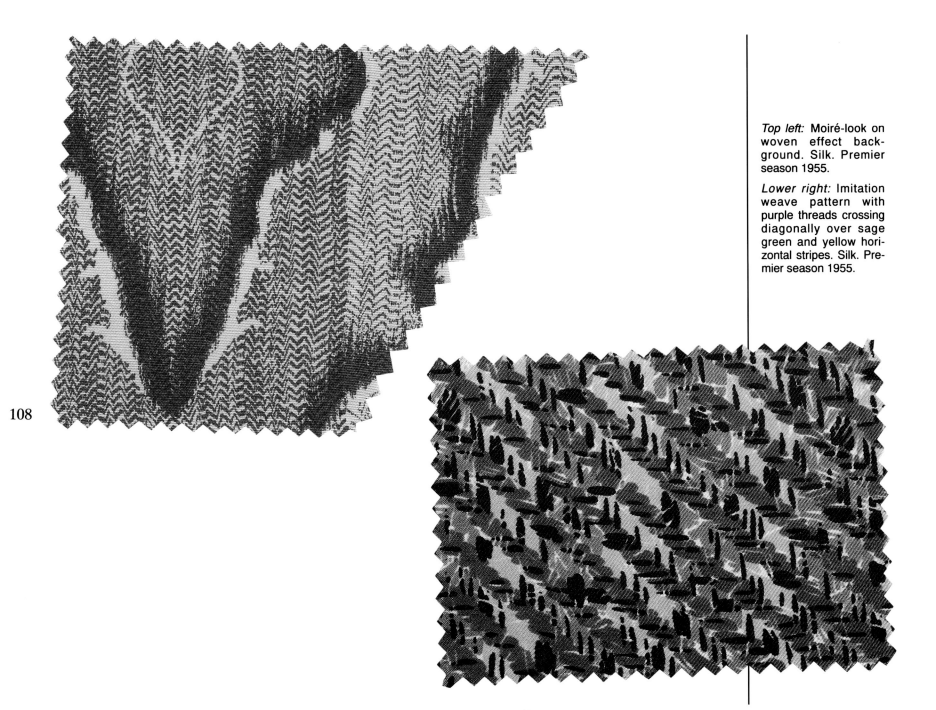

108

Top left: Moiré-look on woven effect background. Silk. Premier season 1955.

Lower right: Imitation weave pattern with purple threads crossing diagonally over sage green and yellow horizontal stripes. Silk. Premier season 1955.

Novelty Designs
Special Effects - Texture

Top: Textured look in soft pastel blue. Silk. Second season 1956.

Center left: Little dabs of color with black shadows in a randomly placed design. Closer examination reveals an orderly pattern with a textured look. Stamped *Fond Nouveau*, "new for the season." Silk. Premier season 1955.

Lower right: Multicolor mosaic pattern with a textured effect, in bold green, magenta, bronze, and black. Rayon. First season 1955.

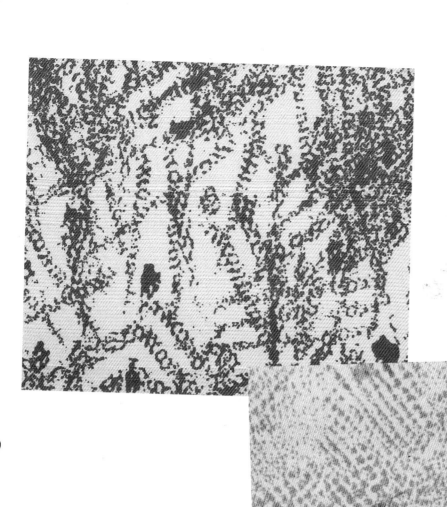

Top left: Heavy woven textured design in dark cherry red. Heavier silk. Second season 1955.

Lower right: A scattering of bright flowers on a multiple textured-look background. Medium-weight cotton. Second season 1955.

Top left: Trompe l'oeil plissé in gray and white checks, a *camaïeu*-style monochromatic print. *Plissé* is taken from the French word meaning wrinkled, and resembles seersucker. Rayon. First season 1955.

Center left: Camaïeu design in monochromatic blue, with the *trompe l'oeil* look of moiré taffeta. Cotton. Premier season 1955.

Lower right: Stylized florals on *trompe l'oeil* brick ground. Note the use of bright blue and tiny touches of yellow. Silk faille. Second season 1955.

Novelty Designs
Special Effects - Trompe L'oeil

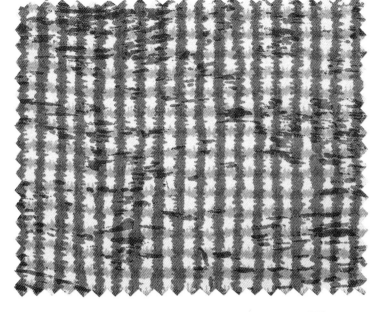

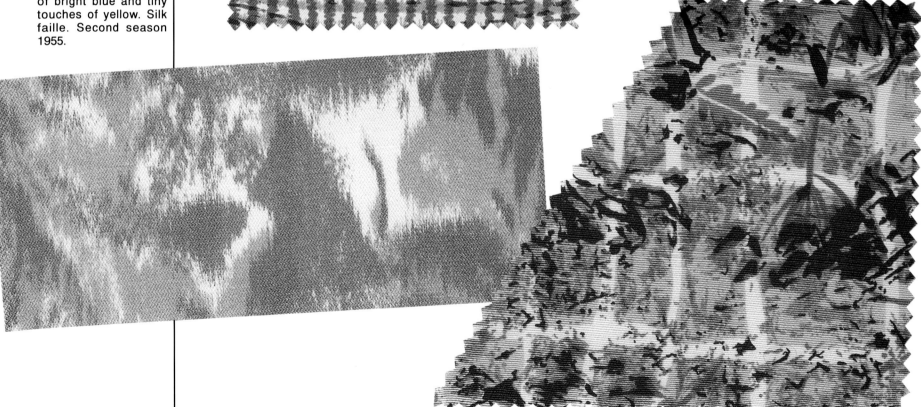

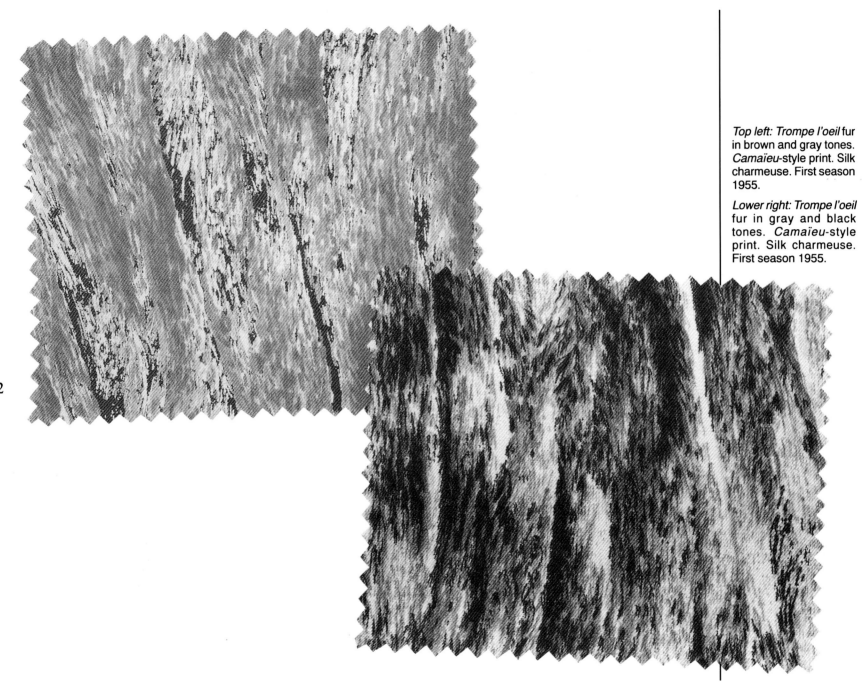

Top left: Trompe l'oeil fur in brown and gray tones. *Camaïeu*-style print. Silk charmeuse. First season 1955.

Lower right: Trompe l'oeil fur in gray and black tones. *Camaïeu*-style print. Silk charmeuse. First season 1955.